Series 3 Exam

SECRETS

Study Guide
Your Key to Exam Success

Dear Future Exam Success Story:

First of all, **THANK YOU** for purchasing Mometrix study materials!

Second, congratulations! You are one of the few determined test-takers who are committed to doing whatever it takes to excel on your exam. **You have come to the right place.** We developed these study materials with one goal in mind: to deliver you the information you need in a format that's concise and easy to use.

In addition to optimizing your guide for the content of the test, we've outlined our recommended steps for breaking down the preparation process into small, attainable goals so you can make sure you stay on track.

We've also analyzed the entire test-taking process, identifying the most common pitfalls and showing how you can overcome them and be ready for any curveball the test throws you.

Standardized testing is one of the biggest obstacles on your road to success, which only increases the importance of doing well in the high-pressure, high-stakes environment of test day. Your results on this test could have a significant impact on your future, and this guide provides the information and practical advice to help you achieve your full potential on test day.

Your success is our success

We would love to hear from you! If you would like to share the story of your exam success or if you have any questions or comments in regard to our products, please contact us at **800-673-8175** or **support@mometrix.com**.

Thanks again for your business and we wish you continued success!

Sincerely,
The Mometrix Test Preparation Team

Need more help? Check out our flashcards at: http://MometrixFlashcards.com/Series3

Written and edited by the Mometrix Exam Secrets Test Prep Team
Printed in the United States of America

TABLE OF CONTENTS

Introduction

Thank you for purchasing this resource! You have made the choice to prepare yourself for a test that could have a huge impact on your future, and this guide is designed to help you be fully ready for test day. Obviously, it's important to have a solid understanding of the test material, but you also need to be prepared for the unique environment and stressors of the test, so that you can perform to the best of your abilities.

For this purpose, the first section that appears in this guide is the **Secret Keys**. We've devoted countless hours to meticulously researching what works and what doesn't, and we've boiled down our findings to the five most impactful steps you can take to improve your performance on the test. We start at the beginning with study planning and move through the preparation process, all the way to the testing strategies that will help you get the most out of what you know when you're finally sitting in front of the test.

We recommend that you start preparing for your test as far in advance as possible. However, if you've bought this guide as a last-minute study resource and only have a few days before your test, we recommend that you skip over the first two Secret Keys since they address a long-term study plan.

If you struggle with **test anxiety**, we strongly encourage you to check out our recommendations for how you can overcome it. Test anxiety is a formidable foe, but it can be beaten, and we want to make sure you have the tools you need to defeat it.

Secret Key #1 – Plan Big, Study Small

There's a lot riding on your performance. If you want to ace this test, you're going to need to keep your skills sharp and the material fresh in your mind. You need a plan that lets you review everything you need to know while still fitting in your schedule. We'll break this strategy down into three categories.

Information Organization

Start with the information you already have: the official test outline. From this, you can make a complete list of all the concepts you need to cover before the test. Organize these concepts into groups that can be studied together, and create a list of any related vocabulary you need to learn so you can brush up on any difficult terms. You'll want to keep this vocabulary list handy once you actually start studying since you may need to add to it along the way.

Time Management

Once you have your set of study concepts, decide how to spread them out over the time you have left before the test. Break your study plan into small, clear goals so you have a manageable task for each day and know exactly what you're doing. Then just focus on one small step at a time. When you manage your time this way, you don't need to spend hours at a time studying. Studying a small block of content for a short period each day helps you retain information better and avoid stressing over how much you have left to do. You can relax knowing that you have a plan to cover everything in time. In order for this strategy to be effective though, you have to start studying early and stick to your schedule. Avoid the exhaustion and futility that comes from last-minute cramming!

Study Environment

The environment you study in has a big impact on your learning. Studying in a coffee shop, while probably more enjoyable, is not likely to be as fruitful as studying in a quiet room. It's important to keep distractions to a minimum. You're only planning to study for a short block of time, so make the most of it. Don't pause to check your phone or get up to find a snack. It's also important to **avoid multitasking**. Research has consistently shown that multitasking will make your studying dramatically less effective. Your study area should also be comfortable and well-lit so you don't have the distraction of straining your eyes or sitting on an uncomfortable chair.

The time of day you study is also important. You want to be rested and alert. Don't wait until just before bedtime. Study when you'll be most likely to comprehend and remember. Even better, if you know what time of day your test will be, set that time aside for study. That way your brain will be used to working on that subject at that specific time and you'll have a better chance of recalling information.

Finally, it can be helpful to team up with others who are studying for the same test. Your actual studying should be done in as isolated an environment as possible, but the work of organizing the information and setting up the study plan can be divided up. In between study sessions, you can discuss with your teammates the concepts that you're all studying and quiz each other on the details. Just be sure that your teammates are as serious about the test as you are. If you find that your study time is being replaced with social time, you might need to find a new team.

Secret Key #2 – Make Your Studying Count

You're devoting a lot of time and effort to preparing for this test, so you want to be absolutely certain it will pay off. This means doing more than just reading the content and hoping you can remember it on test day. It's important to make every minute of study count. There are two main areas you can focus on to make your studying count:

Retention

It doesn't matter how much time you study if you can't remember the material. You need to make sure you are retaining the concepts. To check your retention of the information you're learning, try recalling it at later times with minimal prompting. Try carrying around flashcards and glance at one or two from time to time or ask a friend who's also studying for the test to quiz you.

To enhance your retention, look for ways to put the information into practice so that you can apply it rather than simply recalling it. If you're using the information in practical ways, it will be much easier to remember. Similarly, it helps to solidify a concept in your mind if you're not only reading it to yourself but also explaining it to someone else. Ask a friend to let you teach them about a concept you're a little shaky on (or speak aloud to an imaginary audience if necessary). As you try to summarize, define, give examples, and answer your friend's questions, you'll understand the concepts better and they will stay with you longer. Finally, step back for a big picture view and ask yourself how each piece of information fits with the whole subject. When you link the different concepts together and see them working together as a whole, it's easier to remember the individual components.

Finally, practice showing your work on any multi-step problems, even if you're just studying. Writing out each step you take to solve a problem will help solidify the process in your mind, and you'll be more likely to remember it during the test.

Modality

Modality simply refers to the means or method by which you study. Choosing a study modality that fits your own individual learning style is crucial. No two people learn best in exactly the same way, so it's important to know your strengths and use them to your advantage.

For example, if you learn best by visualization, focus on visualizing a concept in your mind and draw an image or a diagram. Try color-coding your notes, illustrating them, or creating symbols that will trigger your mind to recall a learned concept. If you learn best by hearing or discussing information, find a study partner who learns the same way or read aloud to yourself. Think about how to put the information in your own words. Imagine that you are giving a lecture on the topic and record yourself so you can listen to it later.

For any learning style, flashcards can be helpful. Organize the information so you can take advantage of spare moments to review. Underline key words or phrases. Use different colors for different categories. Mnemonic devices (such as creating a short list in which every item starts with the same letter) can also help with retention. Find what works best for you and use it to store the information in your mind most effectively and easily.

Secret Key #3 – Practice the Right Way

Your success on test day depends not only on how many hours you put into preparing, but also on whether you prepared the right way. It's good to check along the way to see if your studying is paying off. One of the most effective ways to do this is by taking practice tests to evaluate your progress. Practice tests are useful because they show exactly where you need to improve. Every time you take a practice test, pay special attention to these three groups of questions:

- The questions you got wrong
- The questions you had to guess on, even if you guessed right
- The questions you found difficult or slow to work through

This will show you exactly what your weak areas are, and where you need to devote more study time. Ask yourself why each of these questions gave you trouble. Was it because you didn't understand the material? Was it because you didn't remember the vocabulary? Do you need more repetitions on this type of question to build speed and confidence? Dig into those questions and figure out how you can strengthen your weak areas as you go back to review the material.

Additionally, many practice tests have a section explaining the answer choices. It can be tempting to read the explanation and think that you now have a good understanding of the concept. However, an explanation likely only covers part of the question's broader context. Even if the explanation makes sense, **go back and investigate** every concept related to the question until you're positive you have a thorough understanding.

As you go along, keep in mind that the practice test is just that: practice. Memorizing these questions and answers will not be very helpful on the actual test because it is unlikely to have any of the same exact questions. If you only know the right answers to the sample questions, you won't be prepared for the real thing. **Study the concepts** until you understand them fully, and then you'll be able to answer any question that shows up on the test.

It's important to wait on the practice tests until you're ready. If you take a test on your first day of study, you may be overwhelmed by the amount of material covered and how much you need to learn. Work up to it gradually.

On test day, you'll need to be prepared for answering questions, managing your time, and using the test-taking strategies you've learned. It's a lot to balance, like a mental marathon that will have a big impact on your future. Like training for a marathon, you'll need to start slowly and work your way up. When test day arrives, you'll be ready.

Start with the strategies you've read in the first two Secret Keys—plan your course and study in the way that works best for you. If you have time, consider using multiple study resources to get different approaches to the same concepts. It can be helpful to see difficult concepts from more than one angle. Then find a good source for practice tests. Many times, the test website will suggest potential study resources or provide sample tests.

Practice Test Strategy

If you're able to find at least three practice tests, we recommend this strategy:

1. Take the first test with no time constraints and with your notes and study guide handy. Take your time and focus on applying the strategies you've learned.
2. Take the second practice test open-book as well, but set a timer and practice pacing yourself to finish in time.
3. Take any other practice tests as if it were test day. Set a timer and put away your study materials. Sit at a table or desk in a quiet room, imagine yourself at the testing center, and answer questions as quickly and accurately as possible.
4. Keep repeating step 3 on a regular basis until you run out of practice tests or it's time for the actual test. Your mind will be ready for the schedule and stress of test day, and you'll be able to focus on recalling the material you've learned.

Secret Key #4 – Pace Yourself

Once you're fully prepared for the material on the test, your biggest challenge on test day will be managing your time. Just knowing that the clock is ticking can make you panic even if you have plenty of time left. Work on pacing yourself so you can build confidence against the time constraints of the exam. Pacing is a difficult skill to master, especially in a high-pressure environment, so **practice is vital**.

Set time expectations for your pace based on how much time is available. For example, if a section has 60 questions and the time limit is 30 minutes, you know you have to average 30 seconds or less per question in order to answer them all. Although 30 seconds is the hard limit, set 25 seconds per question as your goal, so you reserve extra time to spend on harder questions. When you budget extra time for the harder questions, you no longer have any reason to stress when those questions take longer to answer.

Don't let this time expectation distract you from working through the test at a calm, steady pace, but keep it in mind so you don't spend too much time on any one question. Recognize that taking extra time on one question you don't understand may keep you from answering two that you do understand later in the test. If your time limit for a question is up and you're still not sure of the answer, mark it and move on, and come back to it later if the time and the test format allow. If the testing format doesn't allow you to return to earlier questions, just make an educated guess; then put it out of your mind and move on.

On the easier questions, be careful not to rush. It may seem wise to hurry through them so you have more time for the challenging ones, but it's not worth missing one if you know the concept and just didn't take the time to read the question fully. Work efficiently but make sure you understand the question and have looked at all of the answer choices, since more than one may seem right at first.

Even if you're paying attention to the time, you may find yourself a little behind at some point. You should speed up to get back on track, but do so wisely. Don't panic; just take a few seconds less on each question until you're caught up. Don't guess without thinking, but do look through the answer choices and eliminate any you know are wrong. If you can get down to two choices, it is often worthwhile to guess from those. Once you've chosen an answer, move on and don't dwell on any that you skipped or had to hurry through. If a question was taking too long, chances are it was one of the harder ones, so you weren't as likely to get it right anyway.

On the other hand, if you find yourself getting ahead of schedule, it may be beneficial to slow down a little. The more quickly you work, the more likely you are to make a careless mistake that will affect your score. You've budgeted time for each question, so don't be afraid to spend that time. Practice an efficient but careful pace to get the most out of the time you have.

Secret Key #5 – Have a Plan for Guessing

When you're taking the test, you may find yourself stuck on a question. Some of the answer choices seem better than others, but you don't see the one answer choice that is obviously correct. What do you do?

The scenario described above is very common, yet most test takers have not effectively prepared for it. Developing and practicing a plan for guessing may be one of the single most effective uses of your time as you get ready for the exam.

In developing your plan for guessing, there are three questions to address:

- When should you start the guessing process?
- How should you narrow down the choices?
- Which answer should you choose?

When to Start the Guessing Process

Unless your plan for guessing is to select C every time (which, despite its merits, is not what we recommend), you need to leave yourself enough time to apply your answer elimination strategies. Since you have a limited amount of time for each question, that means that if you're going to give yourself the best shot at guessing correctly, you have to decide quickly whether or not you will guess.

Of course, the best-case scenario is that you don't have to guess at all, so first, see if you can answer the question based on your knowledge of the subject and basic reasoning skills. Focus on the key words in the question and try to jog your memory of related topics. Give yourself a chance to bring the knowledge to mind, but once you realize that you don't have (or you can't access) the knowledge you need to answer the question, it's time to start the guessing process.

It's almost always better to start the guessing process too early than too late. It only takes a few seconds to remember something and answer the question from knowledge. Carefully eliminating wrong answer choices takes longer. Plus, going through the process of eliminating answer choices can actually help jog your memory.

Summary: Start the guessing process as soon as you decide that you can't answer the question based on your knowledge.

How to Narrow Down the Choices

The next chapter in this book (**Test-Taking Strategies**) includes a wide range of strategies for how to approach questions and how to look for answer choices to eliminate. You will definitely want to read those carefully, practice them, and figure out which ones work best for you. Here though, we're going to address a mindset rather than a particular strategy.

Your chances of guessing an answer correctly depend on how many options you are choosing from.

How many choices you have	How likely you are to guess correctly
5	20%
4	25%
3	33%
2	50%
1	100%

You can see from this chart just how valuable it is to be able to eliminate incorrect answers and make an educated guess, but there are two things that many test takers do that cause them to miss out on the benefits of guessing:

- Accidentally eliminating the correct answer
- Selecting an answer based on an impression

We'll look at the first one here, and the second one in the next section.

To avoid accidentally eliminating the correct answer, we recommend a thought exercise called **the $5 challenge**. In this challenge, you only eliminate an answer choice from contention if you are willing to bet $5 on it being wrong. Why $5? Five dollars is a small but not insignificant amount of money. It's an amount you could afford to lose but wouldn't want to throw away. And while losing $5 once might not hurt too much, doing it twenty times will set you back $100. In the same way, each small decision you make—eliminating a choice here, guessing on a question there—won't by itself impact your score very much, but when you put them all together, they can make a big difference. By holding each answer choice elimination decision to a higher standard, you can reduce the risk of accidentally eliminating the correct answer.

The $5 challenge can also be applied in a positive sense: If you are willing to bet $5 that an answer choice *is* correct, go ahead and mark it as correct.

Summary: Only eliminate an answer choice if you are willing to bet $5 that it is wrong.

Which Answer to Choose

You're taking the test. You've run into a hard question and decided you'll have to guess. You've eliminated all the answer choices you're willing to bet $5 on. Now you have to pick an answer. Why do we even need to talk about this? Why can't you just pick whichever one you feel like when the time comes?

The answer to these questions is that if you don't come into the test with a plan, you'll rely on your impression to select an answer choice, and if you do that, you risk falling into a trap. The test writers know that everyone who takes their test will be guessing on some of the questions, so they intentionally write wrong answer choices to seem plausible. You still have to pick an answer though, and if the wrong answer choices are designed to look right, how can you ever be sure that you're not falling for their trap? The best solution we've found to this dilemma is to take the decision out of your hands entirely. Here is the process we recommend:

Once you've eliminated any choices that you are confident (willing to bet $5) are wrong, select the first remaining choice as your answer.

Whether you choose to select the first remaining choice, the second, or the last, the important thing is that you use some preselected standard. Using this approach guarantees that you will not be enticed into selecting an answer choice that looks right, because you are not basing your decision on how the answer choices look.

This is not meant to make you question your knowledge. Instead, it is to help you recognize the difference between your knowledge and your impressions. There's a huge difference between thinking an answer is right because of what you know, and thinking an answer is right because it looks or sounds like it should be right.

Summary: To ensure that your selection is appropriately random, make a predetermined selection from among all answer choices you have not eliminated.

Test-Taking Strategies

This section contains a list of test-taking strategies that you may find helpful as you work through the test. By taking what you know and applying logical thought, you can maximize your chances of answering any question correctly!

It is very important to realize that every question is different and every person is different: no single strategy will work on every question, and no single strategy will work for every person. That's why we've included all of them here, so you can try them out and determine which ones work best for different types of questions and which ones work best for you.

Question Strategies

Read Carefully

Read the question and answer choices carefully. Don't miss the question because you misread the terms. You have plenty of time to read each question thoroughly and make sure you understand what is being asked. Yet a happy medium must be attained, so don't waste too much time. You must read carefully, but efficiently.

Contextual Clues

Look for contextual clues. If the question includes a word you are not familiar with, look at the immediate context for some indication of what the word might mean. Contextual clues can often give you all the information you need to decipher the meaning of an unfamiliar word. Even if you can't determine the meaning, you may be able to narrow down the possibilities enough to make a solid guess at the answer to the question.

Prefixes

If you're having trouble with a word in the question or answer choices, try dissecting it. Take advantage of every clue that the word might include. Prefixes and suffixes can be a huge help. Usually they allow you to determine a basic meaning. Pre- means before, post- means after, pro - is positive, de- is negative. From prefixes and suffixes, you can get an idea of the general meaning of the word and try to put it into context.

Hedge Words

Watch out for critical hedge words, such as *likely, may, can, sometimes, often, almost, mostly, usually, generally, rarely,* and *sometimes.* Question writers insert these hedge phrases to cover every possibility. Often an answer choice will be wrong simply because it leaves no room for exception. Be on guard for answer choices that have definitive words such as *exactly* and *always.*

Switchback Words

Stay alert for *switchbacks.* These are the words and phrases frequently used to alert you to shifts in thought. The most common switchback words are *but, although,* and *however.* Others include *nevertheless, on the other hand, even though, while, in spite of, despite, regardless of.* Switchback words are important to catch because they can change the direction of the question or an answer choice.

Face Value

When in doubt, use common sense. Accept the situation in the problem at face value. Don't read too much into it. These problems will not require you to make wild assumptions. If you have to go beyond creativity and warp time or space in order to have an answer choice fit the question, then you should move on and consider the other answer choices. These are normal problems rooted in reality. The applicable relationship or explanation may not be readily apparent, but it is there for you to figure out. Use your common sense to interpret anything that isn't clear.

Answer Choice Strategies

Answer Selection

The most thorough way to pick an answer choice is to identify and eliminate wrong answers until only one is left, then confirm it is the correct answer. Sometimes an answer choice may immediately seem right, but be careful. The test writers will usually put more than one reasonable answer choice on each question, so take a second to read all of them and make sure that the other choices are not equally obvious. As long as you have time left, it is better to read every answer choice than to pick the first one that looks right without checking the others.

Answer Choice Families

An answer choice family consists of two (in rare cases, three) answer choices that are very similar in construction and cannot all be true at the same time. If you see two answer choices that are direct opposites or parallels, one of them is usually the correct answer. For instance, if one answer choice says that quantity x increases and another either says that quantity x decreases (opposite) or says that quantity y increases (parallel), then those answer choices would fall into the same family. An answer choice that doesn't match the construction of the answer choice family is more likely to be incorrect. Most questions will not have answer choice families, but when they do appear, you should be prepared to recognize them.

Eliminate Answers

Eliminate answer choices as soon as you realize they are wrong, but make sure you consider all possibilities. If you are eliminating answer choices and realize that the last one you are left with is also wrong, don't panic. Start over and consider each choice again. There may be something you missed the first time that you will realize on the second pass.

Avoid Fact Traps

Don't be distracted by an answer choice that is factually true but doesn't answer the question. You are looking for the choice that answers the question. Stay focused on what the question is asking for so you don't accidentally pick an answer that is true but incorrect. Always go back to the question and make sure the answer choice you've selected actually answers the question and is not merely a true statement.

Extreme Statements

In general, you should avoid answers that put forth extreme actions as standard practice or proclaim controversial ideas as established fact. An answer choice that states the "process should be used in certain situations, if..." is much more likely to be correct than one that states the "process should be discontinued completely." The first is a calm rational statement and doesn't even make a definitive, uncompromising stance, using a hedge word *if* to provide wiggle room, whereas the second choice is a radical idea and far more extreme.

Benchmark

As you read through the answer choices and you come across one that seems to answer the question well, mentally select that answer choice. This is not your final answer, but it's the one that will help you evaluate the other answer choices. The one that you selected is your benchmark or standard for judging each of the other answer choices. Every other answer choice must be compared to your benchmark. That choice is correct until proven otherwise by another answer choice beating it. If you find a better answer, then that one becomes your new benchmark. Once you've decided that no other choice answers the question as well as your benchmark, you have your final answer.

Predict the Answer

Before you even start looking at the answer choices, it is often best to try to predict the answer. When you come up with the answer on your own, it is easier to avoid distractions and traps because you will know exactly what to look for. The right answer choice is unlikely to be word-for-word what you came up with, but it should be a close match. Even if you are confident that you have the right answer, you should still take the time to read each option before moving on.

General Strategies

Tough Questions

If you are stumped on a problem or it appears too hard or too difficult, don't waste time. Move on! Remember though, if you can quickly check for obviously incorrect answer choices, your chances of guessing correctly are greatly improved. Before you completely give up, at least try to knock out a couple of possible answers. Eliminate what you can and then guess at the remaining answer choices before moving on.

Check Your Work

Since you will probably not know every term listed and the answer to every question, it is important that you get credit for the ones that you do know. Don't miss any questions through careless mistakes. If at all possible, try to take a second to look back over your answer selection and make sure you've selected the correct answer choice and haven't made a costly careless mistake (such as marking an answer choice that you didn't mean to mark). This quick double check should more than pay for itself in caught mistakes for the time it costs.

Pace Yourself

It's easy to be overwhelmed when you're looking at a page full of questions; your mind is confused and full of random thoughts, and the clock is ticking down faster than you would like. Calm down and maintain the pace that you have set for yourself. Especially as you get down to the last few minutes of the test, don't let the small numbers on the clock make you panic. As long as you are on track by monitoring your pace, you are guaranteed to have time for each question.

Don't Rush

It is very easy to make errors when you are in a hurry. Maintaining a fast pace in answering questions is pointless if it makes you miss questions that you would have gotten right otherwise. Test writers like to include distracting information and wrong answers that seem right. Taking a little extra time to avoid careless mistakes can make all the difference in your test score. Find a pace that allows you to be confident in the answers that you select.

Keep Moving

Panicking will not help you pass the test, so do your best to stay calm and keep moving. Taking deep breaths and going through the answer elimination steps you practiced can help to break through a stress barrier and keep your pace.

Final Notes

The combination of a solid foundation of content knowledge and the confidence that comes from practicing your plan for applying that knowledge is the key to maximizing your performance on test day. As your foundation of content knowledge is built up and strengthened, you'll find that the strategies included in this chapter become more and more effective in helping you quickly sift through the distractions and traps of the test to isolate the correct answer.

Now it's time to move on to the test content chapters of this book, but be sure to keep your goal in mind. As you read, think about how you will be able to apply this information on the test. If you've already seen sample questions for the test and you have an idea of the question format and style, try to come up with questions of your own that you can answer based on what you're reading. This will give you valuable practice applying your knowledge in the same ways you can expect to on test day.

Good luck and good studying!

Futures Trading Theory and Basic Functions Terminology

General Theory

Risk and Ownership

A common refrain is that trading in a futures market is essentially the transfer of risk, while trading in a securities market is simply the transfer of ownership. Trading in securities is an essential element of the capital formation process, and confers a fractional ownership interest to the buyer. Futures (and options) trading exists for the purpose of managing risk (hedging) and facilitating investment strategies (speculating). Futures traders rarely take ownership of the underlying commodity upon contract expiry. Futures are a form of derivatives in that the value of each contract is based upon (that is, derived from) an underlying commodity, asset, or form of economic measurement (interest rates, stock indices, currency exchange rates, etc.). Buying traders have a right to receive (and selling traders have an obligation to provide) delivery of the product in exchange for the agreed upon consideration.

Predecessor of the Modern Forward Contract

The predecessor of the modern forward contract was a type of agreement established by agricultural interests in the 19th century. Farmers partnered with merchants to deliver certain products on a certain future date in exchange for an agreed upon fixed price. The farmer thus knew for certain what types of crops he should plant (and in what quantities), and the merchant was assured a supply for sale. The farmer reduced the risk associated with choosing crops and over/under planting, and transferred the sales price risk to the merchant. The merchant, in turn, reduced his risk of not having adequate supply available for sale.

To-Arrive Contract

A to-arrive contract was an early private agreement between a buyer and a seller in which the terms and conditions of the sale and purchase were agreed upon in advance. The contract was actually settled (by exchange of goods and consideration) once the goods arrived (usually by ocean shipment) at the delivery location. As such, a to-arrive contract is essentially a forward contract in which the terms and conditions of the contract are specific to the buyer and the seller (i.e. personalized). To-arrive contracts were introduced in the U.S. as early as the 19th century, but were commonly used in the England cotton trade in the late 18th century.

Evolution of Futures-Type Contract

As the use of forward contracts between farmers and merchants became more widespread and parties' knowledge of and familiarity with these contracts evolved, the practice of trading contracts rather than the underlying commodities emerged. For example, if the market volume of a given product was less favorable than expected, a merchant might seek to transfer a part of the purchase obligation to another merchant who could benefit. However, both parties would still be subject to the risk of counterparty nonperformance.

As the volume and popularity of contracts continued to grow in the mid-19th century, the introduction of exchanges such as the Chicago Board of Trade (CBOT) and the Chicago Mercantile Exchange (CME) led to the development of the modern futures contract. Custom terms and conditions were replaced by standardization, and contract fulfillment was facilitated and enforced by the exchanges. As a result, the risk to a trader associated with contract nonperformance was effectively eliminated.

Introduction of Contract Standardization

In addition to providing a physical facility within which to trade, the early exchanges—principally the Chicago Board of Trade (CBOT) at first and later the Chicago Mercantile Exchange (CME)—introduced contract standardization. Through the use of uniform terms and conditions, traders were granted the ability to buy and sell contracts multiple times to multiple parties prior to expiration, increasing the volume and liquidity of the market.

The primary contract elements that were standardized included:

- the underlying commodity, including specification of grades and quality (and the related premiums and discounts)
- dates of expiry, upon which delivery was required
- contract size and unit of measure (e.g., wheat in bushels of 5,000)

Exchanges also standardized the settlement process and, through affiliated clearing organizations, effectively guaranteed contract performance by serving as a seller to all buyers, and as a buyer to all sellers.

Late 20th Century Contracts

Throughout the latter part of the 20th century, exchanges continued to develop additional futures products wherever a need existed to hedge a financial position. Interest rate futures were first introduced by the CME in 1976 using the rate of U.S. T-Bills. Later, interest products enabled both private enterprises and banks to hedge positions within and between each other, in effect exchanging fixed rate instruments for variable instruments, and vice versa. Eurodollar contracts followed soon after, using the rate of interest applicable to U.S. dollar denominated accounts on deposits overseas. Other futures products include stock index futures (first using the S&P 500), currencies, and metals. Currently, the most common and widely traded futures contracts (and their primary exchanges) are as follows:

1. interest rates – Chicago Board of Trade, Chicago Mercantile Exchange
2. petrochemicals – New York Mercantile Exchange
3. stock indices – Chicago Mercantile Exchange, New York Board of Trade
4. currency exchange rates – New York Board of Trade, Chicago Mercantile Exchange
5. metals – New York Mercantile Exchange
6. agricultural products – Chicago Board of Trade, Chicago Mercantile Exchange, New York Board of Trade, Kansas City Board of Trade

Currency Futures

Currency futures first evolved in the early 1970s as a result of the so-called Nixon Shock. This occurred when the U.S. Congress severed the relationship between the U.S. dollar and the price of gold at the behest of Richard Nixon, the U.S. president at the time. As a result, the rate of exchange of the developed world currencies was free to float (the post-WWII Bretton Woods agreement ensured these rates remained fixed). This created opportunities for futures to be used to mitigate currency exchange risk.

Solutions to Shortcomings of Early Practices

Modern futures markets provided solutions for many of the shortcomings of early practices, including the following:

- lack of adequate storage for contracts settled by delivery
- standardization of product quality (and defined premiums and discounts for quality differences)
- controlled payment methods and terms
- publication of pricing
- guaranteed contract performance (via exchanges and clearing houses)
- standardization of trading practices (via exchange rules and procedures)

The Futures Contract

Futures Contract Characteristics

A futures contract represents an agreement between two parties (buyer and seller) for the sale and purchase of a product (or a commodity or an asset) on a specified future date. This type of contract has three primary characteristics:

1. The buyer and the seller agree to fulfill the contract at a price stipulated at the time the contract is executed.
2. The purpose of the contract is to reduce the risk of adverse price movements (hedge), or to benefit from beneficial price movements (speculate).
3. The contract may be fulfilled at maturity either through delivery of the underlying product or through the creation of a value offset with other contracts.

Futures contracts traded on an exchange are subject to the rules of the exchange, including specifications for margin requirements, contract size, product grades and quality, pricing (minimum tic size), delivery, and settlement.

Similarities and Differences Between Futures and Forward Contracts

Some key similarities and differences between futures and forward contracts are outlined in the table below:

Contract Characteristic	Futures Contract	Forward Contract
Price	Established upon initiation of the contract	Established at any time by agreement of the parties
Maturity	On a specified date in the future	On a specified date in the future
Products	Typically, a commodity or a financial instrument	Any goods or services agreed upon by the parties
Physical Delivery	May be avoided by an offsetting futures transaction (e.g., a close-out); in practice, few contracts result in delivery	Required unless an alternative arrangement is agreed upon by the parties
Standardization	Required as defined by the rules of the exchange	Unique to each transaction and party (e.g., bespoke)

Tradability	Available via an exchange	Not traded via an exchange; may trade over the counter
Settlement	Executed by a clearinghouse which provides guaranty, but requires margin deposits from the parties	Executed as a private transaction by the parties
Regulation	Regulated by the rules of the exchange and the Commodity Futures Trading Commission	Unregulated other than by commercial law

Bespoke Agreement

A bespoke agreement is one in which the terms and conditions are negotiated for each individual agreement. Contract fulfillment is a private transaction between the parties, and there is a risk that either party could fail to fulfill the agreed upon obligations. In contrast, a futures contract is constructed using standardized terms and conditions, and it trades on an exchange. An exchange clearing organization acts as a guarantor with regard to settlement and contract fulfillment, thus minimizing the risk associated with contract abrogation.

Regulation

Other than certain forward foreign exchange contracts, which fall under the auspices of the Commodity Futures Trading Commission (CFTC), forward exchange contracts are considered to be private contracts. They are not subject to regulation beyond the rules of commercial law. To the extent they are traded, transactions take place off-exchange using an over-the-counter (OTC) market.

Offset Provisions

Offsetting or closing out is a process whereby a futures position, either long or short, is settled or liquidated with an equal but opposite transaction prior to contract expiration. For example, a customer who is "long" 100 contracts of July wheat would sell (short) an equal number of July contracts prior to the expiration date. Contracts which are held until the expiration date (or a contractually determined date prior to the formal expiration date) must be fulfilled through delivery or delivery acceptance of the underlying product. If delivery is not part of the contract, it must be settled through a cash transaction. Note that under certain market conditions, it may not be possible to engage in an offset transaction. While such conditions are considered rare, the National Futures Association (NFA) notes in an interpretive notice of risk disclosure regulations that trading in a contract may be suspended for any number of reasons, such as unusual trading patterns, news events, or even exchange system malfunctions.

General Provisions When Futures Contracts Are Not Offset

At the end of the last trading day specified, futures contracts not offset are subject to either delivery or cash settlement. If delivery is required, it is the responsibility of the seller to issue a notice of intent to deliver to the clearinghouse. The seller retains responsibility for meeting the logistical requirements related to delivery completion. The notice of intent to deliver must include all of the essential details of the delivery, such as the date, place, and time of delivery; the specific product grade and weight; and pricing information. Upon receipt of the notice, the clearinghouse is responsible for identifying a buyer and assigning the delivery notice. A clearinghouse typically follows an established, specific protocol to determine the appropriate member firm and assign the delivery to an eligible customer. The clearinghouse then facilitates the delivery by notifying the respective delivering and receiving parties about the delivery, and may serve as an intermediary for product inspection, documentation, and payment.

Clearinghouse

The function of a clearinghouse (also called a clearing organization) is to reconcile trade positions (match sales and purchases) and facilitate settlement, either by receiving and assigning delivery notices or by initiating cash collections and payments. A clearinghouse will regularly (usually at least daily) receive trade information from the exchange members regarding both the members' customer accounts and proprietary trading among the members themselves. Once the data is reconciled, the clearinghouse will assume the role of counterparty for each trade, effectively serving as a guarantor of contract compliance.

Depending upon the rules of the exchange, a clearinghouse will collect the amount of the original margin deposited by customers from each member, either on a gross basis for each customer account, or on a net basis for the net position of all customer accounts. A clearinghouse also provides a similar settlement mechanism for the proprietary transactions between the members themselves.

Clearing and Non-Clearing Exchange Members

Members of an exchange who are also members of a clearing organization are known as clearing members. As a member of a clearing organization, an individual trader or firm is required to maintain separate accounts with the exchange for each individual customer and for proprietary trading. All trading transactions by a clearing member are processed through the clearing organization. A non-clearing exchange member is one who does not hold membership in both an exchange and a clearing organization. A non-clearing member must use the services of a clearing member in order to process executed transactions. Some exchange members may not qualify for membership acceptance with a clearing organization for such reasons as lack of financial strength or limited administrative ability. Reputation and integrity are also important prerequisites for clearing membership.

Basis Grade

Basis grade is the standard definition of quality for a commodity as determined by the rules of an exchange. A lower or higher quality can be substituted for the basis grade, but the difference will be reflected in the price. A greater quality will command a premium, while a lesser quality will necessitate a discount. For example, the contract specifications for soybean futures as listed on the CBOT defines the standard deliverable grade as #2 yellow, which trades at the contract price. The higher quality #1 yellow trades at a $.06 per bushel premium, while the lower quality #3 yellow trades at a $.06 per bushel discount. All three grades are considered deliverable grades.

Contract Market Exchanges and DTEFs

A contract market is a board of trade authorized by the Commodity Futures Trading Commission to conduct trading in futures and options. Examples include the Chicago Board of Trade (CBOT), the Chicago Mercantile Exchange (CME), and the New York Mercantile Exchange (NYMEX), among many others. A derivatives transaction execution facility (DTEF) is a board of trade or market structured to facilitate the trading of derivatives based upon so-called excluded commodities. These trades are executed by non-retail traders who are using designated commercial entities or futures commission merchants (FCMs). Excluded commodities are primarily those that cannot be physically delivered. Examples include interest rates, currency rates, and stock indices.

Characteristics of Successful Futures Market

The key characteristics that lead to a successful futures market for a specific commodity include:

- Volatility in pricing (leading to a need to manage risk): If pricing is inherently stable, then the need for risk management strategies is reduced or eliminated.
- An active underlying cash market: This means there is a large number of widely distributed, active buyers and sellers who are consistently trading significant volumes of products. If a market is efficient, no single participant or group of participants can manipulate the market to gain an unfair advantage.

The Structure of Futures Markets

Normal Market

The term for a normal market condition in futures trading is contango. In centuries past, contango meant continuation. A normal futures market is said to be contango when the price of contracts continuously increases in direct proportion to the length of time remaining until the contract expires. That is, the longer the time remaining until the contract expires, the higher the price of the contract. This pricing difference reflects the normal market condition of greater demand for spot deliveries and close-to-term contracts. However, an additional cause of the pricing difference, especially for agricultural products, is the cost of holding a commodity due to carrying charges. The longer a seller is required to carry a commodity until delivery (at the expiry of the contract), the higher the costs. For example, lean hogs recently listed on the CBOT were priced at 86 cents per pound for delivery in February. This cost rose to 90 cents per pound for delivery in April, to 97 cents per pound for delivery in May, and to 98 cents per pound for delivery in June or July.

Carrying Charges

The three most commonly cited components of carrying charges are storage, insurance, and financing. The impact these components will have on a carrying charge will vary depending upon the type of commodity the contract is for. The overall cost of managing livestock or holding railcars of ethanol, for example, could involve significant storage and insurance costs, in addition to financing costs. In contrast, holding a financial instrument such as equity securities or government bonds may involve financing costs only. Commodities that are cash settled and are therefore never delivered (such as stock indices, currencies, and interest rates) would typically have few if any carrying charges. In a normal market, the difference between the spot or cash price and the price of a futures contract should be approximately equal to the cost of carry. For example, a January quote on the CBOT for a February contract for lean hogs was 86 cents per pound. The next contract was for April delivery; the price was 90 cents per pound. Therefore, the two-month cost of carry can be inferred to be 4 cents per pound. This example is illustrative but not definitive, as other factors—most importantly supply and demand—also affect the price.

Carrying Costs

A full carry market exists when the difference in price between two contracts that are identical with the exception of their maturity dates is equal to the carrying costs. Futures contracts in which the only carrying charge is interest are typically for financial instruments such as government bonds. In order to accurately estimate the cost of carry, an appropriate measure of the short-term cost of money is required. The rate often used is called the repurchase (repo) rate, which is quoted at a slight premium over the 13-week U.S. Treasury Bill. A full carry market is one in which the price difference between equal contracts with different expiry dates is equal to the interest cost based on the repo rate. Or, calculated another way, the ratio of the price of the long-term contract to the near-term contract should be approximately equal to the repo rate.

Full Carry

Full carry is as much a concept as it is a reality. A market could be above or below full carry despite expectations to the contrary. Consider the following example that uses quotes for cheese futures from the CME:

PRICE QUOTES		CONTRACTS COMPARED	
FEB	1.812	AUG	1.861
MAR	1.820	FEB	1.812
APR	1.830		
MAY	1.830	RATIO:	1.027
JUN	1.850	IMPLIED RATE:	2.70%
JUL	1.857		
AUG	1.861	**ANNUALIZED:**	**5.41%**

Since cheese is a cash-settled commodity, the only cost of carry should be interest. However, the annualized interest rate calculated above is substantially higher than the prevailing rates. Therefore, the market can be considered above full carry, and other factors are affecting the price. Factors influencing the price may include weak supply or strong demand (both for production and consumption), seasonality (and weather), and even trader demographics. For example, large, sophisticated traders are typically more efficient than their smaller counterparts. This difference results in lower transaction costs for one and higher transaction costs for the other. In addition, the rules of the exchange may limit the types of trades available to market participants. For instance, there may be restrictions on short sales.

Inverted Market and Backwardation

The term for an inverted market condition in futures trading is backwardation. A futures market is said to be in backwardation when there is an inverse relationship between the price of contracts and the length of time remaining until contract expiry. That is, the longer the time remaining until contract expiry, the lower the price of the contract. Graphs of an inverted market and a normal or contango market would be mirror images of each other. A backwardation condition may exist during periods of unbalanced supply and demand. The near-term supply of a commodity may be limited (and pricing at a premium), while the long-term supply of the same commodity may be forecast to be plentiful. An inverted market for financial instruments may exist during periods of inverted yield curves. That is, the short-term cost of funds is greater than the long-term cost, resulting in higher prices for shorter-term instruments.

Hedging Theory

Hedged and Unhedged Positions

A hedged position is one that offsets potential losses that may be incurred in a particular investment. Generally, this involves purchasing derivatives (options, collars, straddles, or shorts). Because the investor has to pay for these additional positions, if the underlying investment increases, his or her gains will not be as much as they would have been had they been unhedged; however, the real benefit is in the downside as the investor stands to lose much less than he or she would have otherwise.

Market timing attempts to predict future market prices so that the investor can make short-term gains in their portfolios. Day traders and hedge fund managers often employ this technique in their accounts.

Short sales involve selling a position that one actually does not own. In a short sale, the broker is lending the stock to the customer to sell. The investor must buy back the shares and return them to the broker. The reason investors would employ this technique is if they believe prices are going to drop and that they will be able to buy the position for less than they sell it, enabling them to pocket a small gain.

Future Expectations

The theory of efficient markets holds that the price of a given commodity reflects all known information, which therefore means that the commodity is fairly valued. This would approximate the normal market condition in futures. In a normal market condition, the difference between spot or cash prices and futures contracts is solely the result of carrying costs. In this case, market participants need not consider futures contracts, as the spot price will always be the best price. Reality is, of course, quite different from theory, as future events cannot be predicted. Traders can use expectations or the probability of future events to determine the feasibility of entering into a hedge. For example, the price of oil can fluctuate significantly due to global events. Major consumers of refined oil products (such as airlines) use a hedge to offset the risk that unforeseen events (such as political disruptions or adverse weather) may restrict the supply of oil

Spot Price of Commodities

Hedging tends to reduce the volatility of spot pricing by reducing demand in the cash market. The use of a hedge by a trader prevents panic buying in the case of unforeseen events. If, for example, catastrophic events caused the supply of a commodity to become drastically limited, the spot price would be expected to increase in an equally dramatic fashion. If the buyers and sellers of a commodity do not have a hedge in this type of situation, the buyer will suffer and the seller will benefit. However, if the market participants have hedged their positions, there will be no need for spot buying, and price swings are thereby moderated.

Short Hedge

A short hedge is, in effect, the counterparty to a long hedge, the holder of which often owns the underlying commodity. In a short hedge, a trader seeks to limit exposure to a decline in prices, and thus sells a contract. Unlike the long trader who may foresee future price increases, the short trader is concerned with the possibility of prices actually falling below the futures price. For example, a farmer producing oats may be concerned that an abundant yield will drive future prices lower. Concurrently, a grain company that requires oats in order to produce breakfast cereal may need to lock in a future price to hedge against adverse events. In this case, the grain company enters into a long position and buys a contract to establish price certainty, while the farmer creates a short position to lock in an acceptable sales price.

Long Hedge

Long hedge can be viewed as a type of insurance policy since the transaction cost of the hedge is minimal. To understand how long hedges are used, consider a hypothetical cereal company that requires a steady supply of oats with which to create a consumable finished product. The availability of oats is highly dependent upon weather due to yield variability and transportation costs via river barge. The company can buy oats at the spot price of $3.33 per bushel, which is considered to be within a profitable range. However, at any price above $3.50 per bushel, the cost of production would exceed the price consumers are willing to pay for the cereal. The company has facilities to store about three months of supply. A contract for delivery of oats three months down the road is quoted on the CBOT at a price of $3.44 per bushel. The company is concerned that drought conditions may be more severe than predicted. So, to hedge this risk, the company buys enough three-month contracts to cover its production requirements. As the contract nears expiration, rainfall levels are lower than expected, and the spot price of oats rises to $3.60 per bushel. The cereal company can either wait and take delivery at $3.44 or sell equal contracts at $3.60 and buy the oats on the spot market. Either way, the hedge will save the company $0.16 per bushel of oats.

Speculative Theory

Speculators

Speculators enter into a transaction for the purpose of obtaining large profits through the assumption of considerable risk. Speculators participate in the market with the objective of profiting from price fluctuations, while hedgers seek to reduce the risk of such price fluctuations on an owned position. Speculators are often the counterparty to a hedge, accepting the price risk (and hoping to profit from it) that a hedger seeks to eliminate. Speculators are investors who do not seek to take ownership of the commodities traded. Hedgers, on the other hand, are typically engaged in the process of producing or consuming the underlying commodities that are hedged. By accepting risk, speculators increase the level of liquidity and capital available in a market.

Use of Margin and Leverage

In order to establish a trading account, an individual is required to deposit sufficient funds with an exchange to satisfy both the initial and ongoing (maintenance) margin requirements, which are defined by the exchange. The amount of margin is adjusted periodically based on the volatility of the underlying commodity, but is always a fraction of the value of a contract. Consider the recent information from the New York Mercantile Exchange (NYMEX) for March sweet light crude oil futures:

- Price: $93.51 per barrel
- Contract Size: 1,000 barrels
- Maintenance Margin Requirements: $4,850 per contract

At current prices, a single contract has a value of $93,510. As a result (and assuming the margin reflects the most recent adjustments by the exchange), a trader can buy or sell a contract that is leveraged at roughly 19 times the investment, a margin requirement of about 5%. In contrast, the margin requirements for an equity trading account are often 50% or more.

Leverage

Margin requirements on futures exchanges are significantly lower than those required for equity trading, usually in the range of 5-20% per contract (depending upon the commodity and the exchange), as opposed to 50% or more for equities. Futures traders can therefore control contracts that are worth as much as 20 times the value of the initial margin investment. For speculators, margins create opportunities for large dollar gains, even when changes in prices are relatively small. In the case of hedging, margins can provide significant amounts of risk exposure at a reasonable cost. Consider the following example in which a hypothetical change in price creates a significantly leveraged return on investment (the investment being the per contract margin amount):

CME QUOTE - WTI CRUDE OIL, FEB DELIVERY		
INITIAL MARGIN REQUIRED:	$5,100	
PRICE:	$93.56	per barrel
CONTRACT SIZE	1,000	barrels
CONTRACT VALUE	$93,560	
VALUE OF $.25 CHANGE IN PRICE	$250	
% CHANGE IN CONTRACT VALUE:	0.27%	
RETURN ON MARGIN EMPLOYED:	4.90%	
LEVERAGE RATIO:	**18.3**	

Liquidity and Pricing

Speculators often serve as the counterparties to hedgers. In fact, without speculation, traders seeking to hedge would have a difficult time finding someone to accept the transfer of risk. An orderly market requires sufficient volume and liquidity to provide price stability. Speculators are willing to step in and accept this risk. A market without speculators would be thinly traded, which means that traders experience significant fluctuations in pricing, rendering the practice of completing a hedge problematic.

General Futures Terminology

Associated Person

An associated person (AP) is an individual who, acting as an agent, an employee, or another affiliated person of a *futures commission merchant*, an *introducing broker*, a *commodity trading advisor*, or a *commodity pool operator*, is engaged in the trading of futures orders. An AP solicits or receives discretionary accounts, and may also act as a participant or supervise others who are participants in *commodity pools.*

AP Responsibilities

An associated person (AP), also known as an account executive, is typically responsible for customer-facing activities, which include the following:

- documentation of new accounts
- education regarding disclosures, rules, and procedures
- administration of margin calls
- provision of order information such as pricing and execution status
- response to general inquiries and assistance requests

Basis

Basis is the difference between the cash settlement price (also called the spot price) of a commodity or asset and the price specified in a futures contract for an equivalent commodity or asset. The contract used for comparison is typically one in which the underlying commodity or asset has the same or similar characteristics. The maturity date specified in the terms will also be as close as possible to the date for the spot price. Basis can also be calculated and applied to commodities or assets with dissimilar characteristics, such as time periods, delivery locations, and product grades. As the maturity date for a particular futures contract approaches, the basis is proportionately reduced based on the amount of time remaining until the maturity date. This narrowing of the difference between the cash settlement price and the one specified in the futures contract is known as convergence.

Bucketing and Churning

Bucketing refers to an unscrupulous activity in which a broker or dealer confirms an order on behalf of a customer at an agreed upon price, but then executes the order at a more favorable price. The broker/dealer then keeps the difference. For example, assume that a broker confirms a trade price of X, but is able to execute the order at a trade price of $X - 1$. Instead of passing the reduced price on to the customer, the broker keeps the difference. Brokers who typically engage in such practices are known as bucket shops. Such activities are in violation of the NFA Part 2 rules governing the business conduct of members. Churning is the practice of trading by a broker/dealer in the discretionary account of a customer with the sole objective of increasing commissions. The broker/dealer does not give due regard to the effect his or her actions will have on the customer. Such activities are in violation of the NFA Part 2 rules governing the business conduct of members.

Carrying Charges

Carrying charges (also referred to as the cost of carry) are those costs associated with the time period over which a financial instrument is held (usually an interest charge) or the costs incurred from receiving physical possession of a commodity or an asset (such as any interest on borrowed funds, insurance, delivery, storage, and other ancillary costs). The price of a futures contract typically includes (either directly or implicitly) carrying charges. A lack of carrying charges may indicate an arbitrage opportunity. Negative or positive carry exists when the difference between the cash price and the futures price is substantially different than the actual cost of carry. In the case of financial futures, negative carry occurs when the interest cost of holding a financial instrument is greater than the rate of return provided. Conversely, positive carry occurs when the interest cost of holding a financial instrument is less than the rate of return from the instrument.

Exchange and Clearinghouse

An exchange and a clearinghouse are, respectively, the front and back ends of the futures trading process. An exchange has a responsibility (and the attendant regulatory burden) to manage the execution of the trading process on behalf of customers and exchange members. Most, but not all, members of an exchange are also members of an affiliated clearinghouse. A clearinghouse is an organization operated as either a separate but related entity of an exchange or, in the case of the Chicago Mercantile Exchange and the New York Mercantile Exchange, as a separate department within the exchange. A clearinghouse is primarily responsible for reconciling the trade data received from exchange members and initiating financial transactions to settle gains and losses. Clearinghouses also facilitate both the delivery process for hard commodities and the cash settlement of intangible commodities.

Convergence

Convergence refers to the tendency of the basis (the difference between the cash or spot price and an equivalent futures contract price) to grow smaller (i.e. converge) as the maturity date of the contract grows near. Theoretically, the cash price and the futures price will be the same at the date of maturity (i.e. in the delivery month). Because of this tendency, a trader with a future need for a commodity can evaluate the relative cost of buying a futures contract in lieu of purchasing on the spot market and incurring carrying costs. For example, assume a trader needs a commodity in three months. The spot price is X, and the three-month futures contract price is $X + y$. Because of convergence, the effective price of the commodity in three months will be X. Therefore, the variable y can be evaluated in relation to the trader's own carrying costs of purchasing on the spot market. The opposite would be true for the short trader (i.e. the trader would need to decide whether to sell at X or carry the costs and sell in three months at $X + y$).

Commodity Pool and Commodity Pool Operator

A commodity pool is a type of entity, often a trust or a syndicate, that invests the aggregated funds of its participants in commodity-based futures and/or options contracts. The intent of pooling funds is to achieve greater leverage due to size (similar to a mutual fund) and thereby maximize profits. A commodity pool operator (CPO) is an individual or an entity that acts as an associated person on behalf of the pool investors to manage the funds. The CPO may be responsible for investment decisions. Or, such actions may be taken by a separately employed commodity trading advisor (CTA).

Commodity Trading Advisor

A commodity trading advisor is an individual or an entity typically registered with and certified by the National Futures Association (NFA) that offers fee-based advice and/or analyses on commodity-based futures and/or options investing, including forward contracts and swaps.

Deferred Months of a Futures Contract

Deferred months are those that are beyond the current window (i.e. the spot date and the first month) of a futures contract. As an example, a contract with a 120-day maturity can be considered to have three deferred months at the point of inception. It is the time value of these deferred months which serves to create the price differential between the trading and intrinsic value of a contract.

Pit and Ex-Pit

A pit is a designated area of an exchange, often constructed in the form of an arena, where the open outcry method of trading is used. The term ex-pit refers to the consummation of a futures transaction directly between buyer and seller, rather than on the floor of the exchange. For example, a trader who is short a commodity and agrees to accept delivery may work directly with the trader in the long position to determine and agree on the particulars of the delivery. Once completed, the exchange is notified of the agreement and the transaction is said to have taken place ex-pit, or outside of the exchange (or clearinghouse).

FCM and IB

A futures commission merchant (FCM), also known as a commission house or carrying firm, is an individual or organization that is actively engaged in the process of soliciting and accepting orders for futures and options contracts and executing such orders through an exchange. In addition, an FCM maintains an accounting system to establish individual customer accounts and accept payments for orders. An introducing broker (IB) is an individual or an organization that performs the same customer-facing activities as an FCM, but neither accepts nor accounts for customer payments. Therefore, an IB is required to maintain an affiliation or other relationship with an FCM, which will manage customer accounting and payment receipt. If an FCM agrees to act as a guarantor for the activities of an IB, the guarantor FCM must administer the customer accounting and payment receipts. Otherwise, an IB can use the services of any qualified FCM.

First Notice Day

For those exchanges that require delivery following the end of trading, the first notice day (FND) is the earliest day on which a seller can issue a notice of intent to deliver. The FND is typically the day after the last trading day. The seller is not required to issue a notice of intent to deliver on the FND, but cannot issue this notice before the FND. Some exchanges allow trading to continue concurrent with deliveries. For example, the CBOT-traded March 2020 corn futures have an FND of 2/28/2020, but the final trading day is 3/14/2020. In cases where delivery occurs only after the last trading day, the FND is important to a trader, as it may be the final day on which an offset can be initiated in order to liquidate a position and avoid a delivery. However, depending upon the rules of the exchange, a long trader may still sell a contract to offset a position by using a process called retender. In this case, the delivery notice is returned to the clearinghouse and assigned to another buyer.

Floor Broker and Floor Trader

A floor trader (also known as a local) is a person who is granted trading privileges by an exchange and personally engages in open outcry trading on the floor of the exchange for his or her own account. A floor broker (also sometimes known as a commission house broker) is an individual with the same trading privileges as a floor trader who acts on behalf of others. Floor brokers may be employed by a brokerage firm. They may execute orders only for the customers of the firm, or may operate independently (for numerous brokerages).

Forward Contracts and Futures Contracts

A forward contract represents an agreement between a buyer and a seller regarding the terms of sale of specific goods to be delivered on a specific future date. A forward contract can be applied to any agreed upon commercial transaction, the terms and conditions of which are unique to and used only by the buyer and the seller. The motivation of both the buyer and the seller is typically to lock in the terms and conditions to provide certainty of decision. A futures contract is similar to a forward contract in that it also represents an agreement between a buyer and a seller for specific goods, and is settled on a future date. However, futures contracts differ from forward contracts in that they contain standardized terms and conditions, and are typically traded on an exchange. In addition, futures contracts may be settled by delivery of the underlying goods (such as commodities or financial instruments), but are often closed out or liquidated through the purchase or sale of an offsetting contract.

Normal Market and Inverted Market

A normal market can be characterized as one in which the near-term price is less than the long-term or future price. The higher long-term or future price reflects the cost of carry. That is, the longer the term of the contract is, the higher the storage, insurance, and financing costs will be. An inverted market is one with pricing characteristics that are the reverse of a normal market. That is, the prices of near-term contracts are higher than those of contracts with longer maturities. In effect, the cost of carry is negative. Whether a market is normal or inverted is often a function of the effect of economic conditions on the underlying cash commodity. For example, agricultural or other physical products such as metals are subject to near-term supply shortages, with availability increasing over time. This supply-demand imbalance causes shorter-term contracts to be priced higher than longer-term ones. In financial markets, an inverted market is somewhat synonymous with an inverted yield curve for fixed rate instruments. That is, when short-term rates are higher than long-term ones, the prices for shorter-term contracts will be higher than those for longer-term ones.

Limit up/down and Locked Limit

In order to control price volatility, exchanges set limits on the amount a contract price can increase or decrease during a given trading period, usually one day. The limit is defined as the previous trading period settlement price plus and minus a marginal amount.

For example, a recent settlement price for February ethanol contracts on the CME was $2.205. The daily price fluctuation limit was $0.30. Therefore, the minimum and maximum prices set for the following day were $1.905 and $2.505, respectively.

A limit is said to be locked when the price during any given trading session has reached either the lower or upper limit.

Long and Short Positions

A trader is said to be in a long position when:

- An owned inventory position is held (the trader owns an underlying commodity).
- A trader purchases a contract.
- A trader is in a market position whereby the long positions are greater than the short positions (i.e. net long).

A trader is said to be in a short position when:

- No inventory is owned.
- A trader sells a contract.
- A trader is in a market position whereby the short positions are greater than the long positions (i.e. net short).

Position Trader and Day Trader

A market position can be described as either a single contract or multiple contracts that, collectively, create an open position (either long or short) for the purpose of executing a hedging or speculative strategy. The holder of such positions can be described as a position trader. In contrast, a day trader typically has no market position at the end of the trading day, as all trades are initiated and subsequently offset on the same day.

Tender and Retender

A tender is a formal notice required by the rules of an exchange or a clearinghouse whereby a seller indicates his or her intention to make a delivery to a buyer. The notice is provided to the clearinghouse, which then assigns it to a buyer. It is then the responsibility of the seller to arrange for the delivery, which should also comply with the rules of the exchange or clearinghouse. A retender occurs when an exchange permits the recipient of a delivery notice to immediately sell an offsetting futures contract to clear the account position. The buyer would then return the notice to the clearinghouse. In effect, the buyer would retender the previously tendered notice. The clearinghouse would then assign the delivery to another buyer.

Scalping

Scalping is a type of speculative strategy whereby a trader rapidly executes multiple buy and sell orders with the objective of profiting from small variations in price. A scalper is often described as a trader who is prepared to execute a buy order at a fraction below the last transaction price and immediately sell at the next fractionally higher transaction price.

The beneficial effect to the market is the facilitation of liquidity.

Spot Price and Futures Price

The term spot is used to describe either the actual market for immediate purchase and delivery of a commodity or the nearest delivery month of a futures contract. The spot price, then, is the actual cash price applicable to a transaction. The futures price is the price to be paid by a buyer (and received by a seller) for delivery of a commodity on a future date. In a normal market, the price of a futures contract is equal to the spot or cash price plus the cost of carry.

Variation Call

A variation call is issued by a clearinghouse to a member when the net position value of the member and, separately, each customer of the member, falls below the maintenance margin requirements. The subsequent payment to restore the maintenance margin is the variation margin amount. For example, consider the recent information from the New York Mercantile Exchange (NYMEX) for March sweet light crude oil futures:

- Price: $93.51 per barrel
- Contract Size: 1,000 barrels
- Maintenance Margin Requirements: $4,850 per contract

Assuming the margin amount above reflects the latest adjustments by the exchange and the trader holds one contract, a $1 decline in the price per barrel would create a $1,000 loss to the trader, which is charged to the trader's account. If the subsequent value of the account falls below $4,850, a variation call would be issued to the trader in the amount required to restore the value of the account to the maintenance margin amount.

Warehouse Receipt

For contracts that are held to expiry and require physical delivery, the clearinghouse may operate as the facilitator of the delivery process and assume the role of depository for warehouse receipt. The actual warehouse receipt document(s) is/are issued by a warehouse that is recognized by the clearinghouse as being certified for such delivery purposes. The document is provided to the clearinghouse to complete the delivery process and authorize release of payment to the seller as provided by the purchaser.

General Options Terminology

At the Money, in the Money, and out of the Money

At any time, a comparison of the strike price of an option and the price of the underlying security will yield one of three results, as indicated in the following example:

Price				
Security	**Strike**	**Difference**	**Calls**	**Puts**
$25	$20	$5	In the money	Out of the money
$20	$20	$--	At the money	At the money
$15	$20	$ (5)	Out of the money	In the money

Note the inverse relationship between calls and puts.

The phrases ending in "the-money" describe the position of an option as it approaches the strike price of the contract. Depending on the type of contract, the phrase "in-the-money" describes an option in which the price of a security has moved past the strike price, and the option may be exercised for a profit. The phrase "out-of-the-money" describes a security price that has moved past the strike price such that the option has no value. The phrase "at-the-money" describes a security price that matches the strike price of an options contract, and at any point following the strike price it would make sense to exercise an option. For example, the holder of a call option with a strike price of $35 on ABC stock would be out-of-the-money when the price of ABC reached $34, at-the-money at $35, and in-the-money at $36 (depending on the premium they paid).

Call and Put

A call option represents the right to purchase a specified commodity or asset at a specified price within a specified time frame. A trader who purchases a call is said to establish a long market position. A trader who sells a call is said to establish a short market position. A put option represents the right to sell a specified commodity or asset at a specified price within a specified time frame. A trader who buys a put is said to establish a short position with respect to the underlying asset. A trader who sells a put is said to establish a long position with respect to it. This is because a "long position" is one that wants the underlying asset's price to rise, while a short position wants it to decrease.

Conversion

The combination of long and short option positions, as well as similar combinations of both options and futures positions, creates what are known as synthetic positions. Conversion is said to occur when market makers identify a price discrepancy and take an opposite position, which, in turn, causes the pricing to revert to equality. Traders will sell an overpriced call and buy (take a long position) on the futures and the put. A reverse conversion is said to occur when traders buy an underpriced call and sell the futures and the put.

Delta

Delta, also known as the hedge ratio, is a measure of the volatility in the price of an option that is expressed as a value between 0 and 1.0 for calls, and as a value between 0 and -1.0 for puts. In effect, it is the correlation. The measure is derived by comparing the expected change in the price of an option to the change in price of the underlying commodity. Delta can be useful to a trader when he or she is determining the number of option contracts required to hedge a position. For example, a delta with an absolute value of 1.0 indicates a 1:1 match between the number of options required relative to the underlying security. If a trader seeks to hedge a 10,000-share long position and an option contract represents 1,000 shares, the delta would suggest that 10 contracts are required. If the delta was 0.75, on the other hand, 13 contracts would be required.

Exercising

Option contracts give the holder the right but not the obligation to buy or sell an underlying asset at a specified price within a specified time period. Options are exercised when their value is in the money, which occurs when the price of the underlying asset is greater than the strike price of a call option or less than the strike price of a put option.

Consider the following example:

SECURITY PRICE	$25	$20	$15
STRIKE PRICE	$20	$20	$20
DIFFERENCE	$5	$0	-$5
CALL OPTION	in the money	at the money	out of the money
ACTION	***Exercise***		
PUT OPTION	out of the money	at the money	in the money
ACTION			***Exercise***

Expiration is the date after which an option will expire if it is not exercised.

Grantor and Writer

Grantor and writer are two synonymous terms for an individual or entity that creates and issues for sale (in exchange for a premium) an option contract. This individual or entity is obligated to fulfill the terms of the contract if an option is exercised. A grantor or writer of a put option is obligated to purchase the underlying commodity, while a grantor or writer of a call option is obligated to sell the underlying commodity.

Intrinsic Value

As it relates to options pricing, intrinsic value is the difference between the strike price of an option and the current price of the underlying security. This is commonly referred to as the "in the money" amount. For example, if the strike price of a call option is $25 and the current price of the security is $30, the option is considered to be in the money by $5, which is its intrinsic value. Likewise, if the strike price of a put option is $25 and the price of the security is $15, the put has an intrinsic value of $10. Note that negative values are typically expressed as zero. For example, a put option with a strike price of $25 and a security price of $30 has zero intrinsic value.

Time Value

Broadly defined, intrinsic value is the difference between the strike price of an option and the price of the underlying asset. At expiration, an option is worth only its intrinsic value. For example, if a security is priced at $25 on an option expiration day and the strike price of the option is $20, the value of the option is $5. This is because paying $5 to purchase at $20 is the same as purchasing at $25 at market. However, during the life of the option prior to expiration, the element of time will impact the value of the option. For example, if there is a long period of time remaining until expiry, an option will typically command a premium because there is greater opportunity (i.e. time) for a favorable outcome. In this case, the option value will be greater than the intrinsic value. A second component related to time value is the volatility of the underlying commodity. Large price fluctuations over the life of an option period also result in pricing premiums, as the condition results in both opportunity for the holder of the option and compensation for the writer of the option.

Spread, Straddle, and Strangle

Spreads, straddles, and strangles are trading strategies designed to minimize risk due to adverse changes in the prices of underlying commodities. Each involves a combination of long and short positions that use either futures contracts and options (for spreads) or options alone (for straddles and strangles). Spread example: A trader seeking to hedge a long position might purchase both a related futures contract and a put. If prices of the underlying commodities fall, the put can be exercised. If prices rise, gains are available from the futures. If prices remain relatively unchanged, the loss to the trader is limited to the premium paid for the put. A straddle is a similar strategy involving the purchase of either two put options or two call options, each having the same expiration date and strike price.

A strangle is similar to a straddle in that the expiration dates of the puts or calls are the same, but the strike prices are different.

Synthetic Positions

The combination of long and short option positions as well as similar combinations of both options and futures positions creates what are known as synthetic positions. That is, the combination creates a position that mimics that of a single futures position. The six option/future combinations that create synthetic positions are as follows:

$$\begin{aligned} \text{Long Call} &= \text{Long Futures} + \text{Long Put} \\ \text{Short Call} &= \text{Short Futures} + \text{Short Put} \\ \text{Long Put} &= \text{Short Futures} + \text{Long Call} \\ \text{Short Put} &= \text{Long Futures} + \text{Short Call} \\ \text{Long Futures} &= \text{Long Call} + \text{Short Put} \end{aligned}$$

Short Futures = Short Call + Long Put

A synthetic position is created by purchasing or selling a combination of two option or futures positions, which together can provide the same result as a single actual futures position. Synthetics have value to a trader when a discrepancy exists between the price of the actual position and the price of the synthetic position. For example, if a trader requires a long call position to establish a hedge, two alternatives are available. The first is an actual long call, and the second is a synthetic long call, which is a combination of a long futures contract and a long put. If the price of the synthetic long call is less than the price of the actual position, the trader could purchase the synthetic and achieve the desired hedge position at a lower cost.

Futures Margins, Option Premiums, Price Limits, Futures Settlements, Delivery, Exercise, and Assignment

Margin Requirements

Margin Requirements for Futures Traders

Margin requirements are established by each individual exchange, and they vary based upon the underlying commodity supporting the contract. Brokers may require higher margins of their customers than those set by an exchange, but these margins can never be lower than the ones set by an exchange. Various statistical analyses are used by exchanges to measure price volatility and set margin requirements accordingly. The amount of margin required is set at a per contract level. At this set level, traders can be expected to cover any probable losses in the case of normal price fluctuations. For example, margins on the Chicago Mercantile Exchange (CME) are expected to be sufficient to cover as much as 99% of the probable price changes during a given trading day or multiple trading days. Changes in the underlying factors that can cause price volatility (supply disruptions, conflicts, disasters, government policy, etc.) are monitored, and margin levels are adjusted as volatility is affected.

Performance Bond

Margins used in futures markets are called performance bonds because their purpose is to function as a form of surety or earnest deposit to demonstrate good faith intent regarding contract execution. Both counterparties to a contract (i.e. both long and short positions) require futures margins. In contrast, margins established for trading in equity securities are a form of cash down payment. The balance is due (and ownership is transferred) at a later date. For futures transactions, most contracts are settled with offsetting trades, not through delivery of the underlying commodity.

Initial Margin and Maintenance Margin

The amount of initial margin is that which is required to open a trading account and establish a market position. Thereafter, if a trader experiences adverse changes that reduce the account value below a certain level, additional funding (often called a margin call) is required. This maintenance margin amount is the minimum that must remain on deposit over the life of the account, and is analogous to a minimum balance required for a bank account. For example, the recent margin levels required to trade cocoa and coffee on the NYMEX were set as indicated below:

Product	Start Period	End Period	Initial	Maintenance
NYMEX COCOA	Mar-15	Dec-16	1,870 USD	1,700 USD
NYMEX COFFEE	Mar-15	Dec-16	4,950 USD	4,500 USD

Margin requirements set by an exchange are a function of the price volatility of the underlying commodity, not only current and historic volatility, but also volatility that is expected in the future. For example, the Chicago Mercantile Exchange (CME) sets maintenance margins at a level sufficient to provide funding for 99% of the probable price change in a commodity during a given day or over a series of days. Initial margins are a function of maintenance margins, and are usually a certain percentage higher than maintenance margins (though this relationship can also be reversed). For example, recent maintenance margins at the CME for EUR/USD contracts were set at $2,500. The initial margin was 10% higher at $2,750. Margins may also be set at different levels depending upon the trading strategy. For example, speculative account margins are set at a higher level than the margins for hedging accounts.

Margin Agreements

Brokers are required to maintain documentation regarding the terms and conditions of margins. These so-called margin agreements specify the procedures that customers are required to follow to respond to margin requirements. For example, a brokerage may require customers to respond to margin deficiencies the same day such deficiencies are incurred. Other brokers may allow customers to respond to margin deficiencies the following day. Some brokers may accept a check as payment, while others may require payment by wire transfer that is supported by a wire transfer agreement.

SPAN

The growing sophistication of trading strategies employing both futures and options led to the development of portfolio-based risk assessment tools for margin requirements. The current industry standard is a tool called Standard Portfolio Analysis of Risk (SPAN), which was developed by the Chicago Mercantile Exchange (CME). Using SPAN, the overall portfolio risk of a position is determined by calculating the gains and losses that a portfolio could be expected to incur under various market conditions. The results are used to identify the worst possible loss that a portfolio of derivative and physical instruments might reasonably incur over a specified time period (usually a single trading day). This worst loss scenario serves as the basis for an evaluation of the adequacy of existing margin requirements and the need for modifications.

Net Liquidating Value Component

As the term implies, the net liquidating value component represents the value of both the futures and options components of a portfolio in the event of liquidation. The calculation includes three elements: cash on deposit, unrealized profit/loss on open futures positions, and net value of open option positions.

Consider the following example:

CASH ON DEPOSIT					**$ 60,000.00**
OPEN FUTURES POSITIONS					
Qty	Per Contract	Commodity	Price	Settle	Gain/ (Loss)
10	5,000	LONG MARCH SOYBEANS	$ 14.18	$ 14.12	(3,000.00)
2	60,000	SHORT MAY SOYBEAN OIL	$ 0.4924	$ 0.4614	3,720.00
					$ 720.00
NET OPTION VALUE					
5	€ 125,000	EUR/USD CALL MARCH	0.0220	0.0183	**$ (2,312.50)**
NET LIQUIDATING VALUE					**$ 58,407.50**

Risk Array

Using parameters established by the exchange and/or clearing organization, the SPAN tool calculates a series of portfolio profit/loss scenarios that is termed a risk array. A typical calculation produces 16 such scenarios, each of which is based on specific assumptions, examples of which are as follows:

- futures down 1/3 of range; volatility up
- futures down 1/3 of range; volatility down
- futures down 2/3 of range; volatility up
- futures down 2/3 of range; volatility down

Calculations based upon each assumption (both short and long positions) result in a potential gain or loss. The largest potential loss position is compared to the net liquidating value to assess any required margin adjustments.

Equity Amounts

A margin call requires a trader to immediately increase the funds or collateral on deposit as a performance bond. In the same way that a loss of funds that causes the value of an account to drop below the maintenance margin requirement must be compensated for with a deposit, any amounts that exceed the maintenance margin requirement (so-called equity amounts) may be withdrawn from the account.

Margin Requirements for Hedge and Speculative Accounts

Due to the inherent differences in trading strategy risk, margins for speculators are typically set at a premium compared to those for hedgers. For example, recent initial margins for corn futures traded on the CBOT were set at $2,700 for speculators and at $2,000 for hedgers. Traders typically engage in hedging only in those markets in which a cash position is maintained. That is, trading is intended to protect the value of an existing inventory or cash position. The risk of such activity is much lower than that associated with speculative trades, and this risk is further reduced by the ability of the hedger to make or accept delivery if the contract is held until the expiration date.

Spread and Spread Margin

A spread position is created as a result of the concurrent purchase and sale (long and short positions) of related but not identical contracts. The spread margin is the amount required to establish and maintain spread trading. Since the price volatility of the two positions combined can be expected to remain lower than that of each position separately, the spread margin requirements are lower as well. Calculating a spread margin requires that the following variables be considered: outright margin, spread credit, and contract ratio.

Consider the following example:

SOYBEAN MEAL CALENDAR SPREAD	Outright Margin	Contract Ratio	Total Margin	Spread Credit	Spread Margin
1 LONG SOYBEAN MEAL	$ 2,000	1	$ 2,000	87.5%	$ 250
1 SHORT SOYBEAN MEAL	$ 2,000	1	$ 2,000	87.5%	$ 250
			$ 4,000		**$ 500**

The formula to calculate the spread margin is as follows:

[Leg 1: Outright Margin × Contract Ratio × (1 – Spread Credit)]

+ [Leg 2: Outright Margin × Contract Ratio × (1– Spread Credit)]

Outright Margin, Spread Credit, and Contract Ratio

These terms are applicable to the calculation of margin requirements for spread contracts, and are defined as follows:

- Outright margin is simply the maintenance margin, and is calculated as if each of the legs of the spread were traded separately. If the contract is being traded speculatively, the margin is calculated as the hedge maintenance margin increased by a specific factor.
- Spread credit is determined by the exchange, and represents the rate of reduced-price volatility for the two positions trading together.
- Contract ratio represents the ratio of the number of contracts to each leg of the spread.

Option Premiums

Intrinsic Value, Time Value, and Option Premium

Intrinsic value is the difference between the strike price of an option and the price of the underlying security. If the option is a call, intrinsic value exists if the price of the security is greater than the strike price. If the option is a put, intrinsic value exists if the price of the security is lower than the strike price. A negative intrinsic value is expressed as zero.

If the price of an option is greater than the calculated intrinsic value, the option can be said to have time value. That is, the length of time until the option expires represents an opportunity for the price of the underlying security to move in a favorable direction. This opportunity is reflected in the price of the option.

An option premium is the amount received by the writer or seller of the option from the buyer, and represents the sum of the intrinsic value and the time value.

These relationships are illustrated in the following table:

SECURITY PRICE	\$25	\$20	\$15
STRIKE PRICE	\$20	\$20	\$20
DIFFERENCE	\$5	\$0	-\$5
INTRINSIC VALUE:			
CALL	**\$5**	\$0	
PUT		\$0	**\$5**
IF OPTION PRICE IS:	\$7		\$7
TIME VALUE IS:	**\$2**		**\$2**
INTRINSIC VALUE	\$5		\$5
+ TIME VALUE	\$2		\$2
= PREMIUM (PRICE PAID TO SELLER)	**\$7**		**\$7**

Option Delta

As the term is used in option pricing, option delta refers to the relationship between changes in the price of an option and the price of the underlying asset. This relationship can be used to try to quantify how the price of an option will change when there is a change in the value of the underlying asset. For example, a delta of 0.50 or 50% indicates that a \$10 change in the value of an asset will cause a corresponding \$5 change in the value of the option. A delta of zero would indicate that there is no relationship between the price of an option and the price of an asset. Conversely, a delta of 1.0 or 100% would represent a 1:1 relationship; a \$1 change in the price per asset = a \$1 change in the price per option. An option delta can be useful when constructing hedge positions, because it can be used to predict the expected change in option price (and thus the number of contracts required) relative to the underlying asset to be hedged. Speculators find value in the delta in the same fashion, as they trade in options based on expectations of changes in the underlying asset.

Premium Value

The following quotation is from the CME. The option for Euro FX is highlighted in white.

CALLS					PUTS			
Bid Size	Bid Price	Ask Price	Ask Size	Strike Price	Bid Size	Bid Price	Ask Price	Ask Size
10	0.0172	0.0182	10	1.3100	150	0.0021	0.0023	60
35	0.0134	0.0141	35	1.3150	183	0.0032	0.0034	35
15	0.0103	0.0105	65	1.3200	100	0.0048	0.0050	84

The premium represents the price paid to the writer or seller of the option. In the example above, the premium is the bid price. For the call, the bid is quoted at 0.0134 cents per unit of Euro; for the put, the bid is quoted at 0.0032 cents per unit of Euro. A standard contract consists of €125,000, bringing the premium value to \$1,675 for the call and \$400 for the put.

European Style Option and American Style Option

An option contract is said to be European style if the contract must be held until the maturity date in order be exercised. In contrast, an American style option can be exercised at any point during the period prior to the expiration date. Because of this feature, American style options tend to be priced at a premium compared to European style options. This premium reflects the additional exercise flexibility.

Value of Single Bond

U.S. Treasury bond prices are quoted as a percentage of par plus points of 1/32. A price of 146-17 represents 146 (or 146%) of par value plus 17/32 (or 0.53125%) of par value (par = $100,000). The price of the bond is therefore 146.53125% of par, which is equal to $146,531.25.

Value of a Single Note

U.S. Treasury note prices are quoted as a percentage of par plus points of 1/32 and halves of 1/32. A price of 110-065 represents 110% of par value plus 6.5/32 (or 0.203125%) of par value (par = $100,000). The price of the note is therefore 110.203125% of par, which is equal to $110,203.12.

Discount Rate and Value of a Single Bill

U.S. Treasury bills are quoted as 100 minus the discount rate of the delivery month. At a price of 99.27, the discount rate is calculated as 100 – 99.27, or 0.73%. The contract standard is a single 13-week T-Bill with a face value of $1,000,000. Therefore, the contract value is $992,700. Note that T-Bill futures contracts are cash settled transactions, unlike bonds and notes that are settled with delivery. In the contract above, if the final settlement price is set at 98.85, the position would be settled with a gain of $1,050 as follows:

$\$1,000,000 \times 90/360 \times (0.9927 - 0.9885) = \$1,050$

Price Limits

Locked Limit

Daily price limits are expressed in terms of a fixed amount above or below the current closing price of a contract. A price is said to have reached its locked limit when it has risen or fallen to its upper or lower limit amount. At this point, all trading in the contracts is suspended until the following day. However, limits can be adjusted based on the rules of the exchange. Since price limits exist to control panic buying and selling, the factors underlying a locked limit are examined to ascertain any such behavior. For example, if volatility is a result of the natural behavior of traders as an expiration period approaches (buying and selling to unwind positions), the limits may be adjusted so that trading can resume.

Based on the following CME quote for soybeans, at what price would a contract reach its locked limit if the daily limit is $0.70 per bushel?

Month	Last	Change	Prior Settle	Open	High	Low	Volume
Jan 2016	1430'2	+21'4	1408'6	1408'6	1438'6	1408'4	52,900

Since soybean prices are quoted in cents per bushel and the previous settlement price was 1408-6 cents (or $14.086), the limits for the following day would be set at $14.086 +/- $0.70 (or $13.386 and $14.786).

Circuit Breakers

Circuit breakers are a coordinated, market-wide suspension of trading that first emerged when there were large price changes in the Dow Jones Industrial Average (DJIA). Such trading interruptions are designed to provide a "cooling off" period, during which market participants can reassess their trading strategies. This allows for the reestablishment of a more balanced trading environment within the market. Exchanges such as the Chicago Mercantile Exchange (CME) have adopted the same circuit breakers in futures and options contracts using stock indices as the underlying measure. For example, the CME recently established DJIA circuit breakers at 1300, 2650, and 3950 points, which represent index changes of 10%, 20%, and 30%. Similar breaks were established for all index-based contracts.

Offsetting Contracts, Settlements, Delivery

Methods to Settle a Futures Contract

Futures contracts can be settled on the contract settlement date through either physical delivery (primarily for hard assets such as agricultural products and metals, but also for treasury notes and bonds) or through a cash payment (for nondeliverables such as interest, currency rates, and stock indices, and also for treasury bills). Liquidation as a form of settlement consists of offsetting trades, also called reversing trades. Examples of offsetting trades include selling to offset a long position or buying to offset a short position. The intent is to revert to a zero position, though getting to a position of exactly zero is not always possible. Offsets are by far the most prevalent method of settling a futures contract.

Contracts that are settled through cash payments are, in most cases, those that have underlying commodities or assets that are intangible, such as stock indices or interest rates. However, many other types of contracts also require cash settlement, examples of which include the following [based on recent settlement data from the Chicago Mercantile Exchange (CME)]:

- dairy (butter, cheese, milk, whey)
- weather (temperature, frost, hurricanes)
- currency exchange rates
- federal funds rates
- Eurodollar
- bond indices

The actual settlement process varies depending upon the underlying asset, index, or rate, but typically involves a mark to market process that uses a final settlement price determined by the exchange. Gains and losses are calculated based upon the final settlement price, and the accounts of traders are charged accordingly. Equity can be withdrawn from the account, while funding deficiencies must be restored to maintenance margin levels.

Liquidation

Liquidating (also known as offsetting or closing out) a long or short futures or options contract involves purchasing or selling opposite positions. The risk of liquidating a position arises when the appropriate number of offsetting contracts is either unavailable or unfavorably priced. If the contracts cannot be precisely matched, the trader will not achieve a net zero position through the clearing organization. Instead, the trader will create a new contract obligation while retaining the initial contract.

Measurement of Net Profit or Loss

The close out (or liquidation) of a position creates realized profits and losses based on the price movement of the underlying commodity. Long positions generally benefit from price advances, while short positions benefit from price declines. The simplest form of measurement takes the contract size and the opening and closing price data into account.

Consider the following example:

STANDARD CALCULATION METHOD					
Qty	Per Contract	Commodity	Price	Settle	Gain/ (Loss)
10	5,000	LONG MARCH SOYBEANS	$ 14.18	$ 14.12	(3,000.00)
2	60,000	SHORT MAY SOYBEAN OIL	$ 0.4924	$ 0.4614	3,720.00
					$ 720.00

Both positions experienced a price decline, which resulted in a loss for the long soybeans and a gain for the short soybean oil.

The point method is a type of calculation shortcut whereby the standard quantity per contract is combined with the minimum price fluctuation increment to determine a per contract value.

Consider the following example:

POINT METHOD							
			Fluctuation		Price (cents per unit)		
Qty	Per Contract	Commodity	Pricing Unit	Minimum Contract	Buy	Settle	Gain/ (Loss)
10	5,000	LONG MARCH SOYBEANS	$0.01	$50.00	1418.0	1412.0	(3,000.00)
2	60,000	SHORT MAY SOYBEAN OIL	$0.01	$600.00	49.24	46.14	3,720.00
							$ 720.00

Since each contract has a standard quantity and the pricing is expressed in cents per unit, a contract value per unit can be calculated. The profit or loss is then calculated as the product of three factors:

- change in price (in units)
- minimum contract value change
- number of contracts

For long March soybeans, this is calculated as follows: 6 × $50 × 10. For short May soybean oil, it would be calculated in the following manner: 3.1 × $600 × 2.

Though the point method does not intuitively seem simpler, it is a good shortcut when traders are intimately familiar with the contract specifications for a commodity.

First Notice Day

Though exchange rules may vary, the first notice day is typically the earliest day on which a seller can present an intent to deliver notice. A long trader who waits until after the first notice day to liquidate a contract risks receiving a delivery assignment (to receive delivery) from the exchange, which will complicate the intended close out.

Switching and Rolling

Switching and rolling is a means of offsetting a position as the first notice day draws near. A trader can avoid the risk of a delivery assignment and continue to maintain a long position by simultaneously selling an existing long position (in the spot month) and purchasing an equivalent number of contracts to duplicate his or her original position. Though delivery risk is avoided, the additional trades are associated with additional costs, principally commissions.

Delivery Process

Role of Clearinghouse

The practice of a clearinghouse of assuming the role of counterparty to each trade (as buyer for each seller and as seller for each buyer) serves to facilitate the delivery process for those contracts that will be settled in this manner. Though the clearinghouse guarantees financial performance on each contract, the obligation to ensure that the physical commodity is delivered by the short or the seller remains with the member firm who owns the customer relationship. A clearinghouse will act as an intermediary between the two parties to the contract, receiving delivery notices and subsequently assigning those notices to a buyer. The actual delivery process can take place privately between the parties, or the clearinghouse may continue to be included. If the clearinghouse facilitates the delivery, it will continue to act as the intermediary for documentation and final payment. However, it is the responsibility of the seller to conform to the rules of the exchange and make the logistical arrangements for transferring the commodity.

Warehouse Receipt

A warehouse receipt is a document used in the delivery process that provides evidence of possession of a commodity by a warehouse authorized by the exchange. The document is used by the clearinghouse to confirm delivery by the seller and receipt by the buyer. It also provides authorization for final settlement (and payment) per the terms of the contract.

Complete Contract

Traditionally, a contract is considered complete when delivery is completed (and verified). However, contracts that do not result in delivery (ones that are cash settled) are considered complete when the final settlement price is set by the exchange and each customer account is marked to market.

Retender

Depending upon the rules of a particular exchange, traders who receive a delivery assignment but prefer not to accept delivery may be allowed to sell an offsetting contract. Assuming that the trader is able to achieve an exact offset (i.e. a return to a zero position), the exchange will allow the trader to return the delivery assignment back to the clearinghouse for assignment to another trader, a process known as a retender.

Establishing the Value of a Eurodollar Contract

Eurodollar contracts are based upon a $1 million time deposit with a three-month maturity. The pricing is quoted using the London Interbank Offered Rate (LIBOR) for three months. A 360-day year is also used. A subsidiary of the Chicago Mercantile Exchange (CME), the International Monetary Market (IMM), determines the settlement price using various procedures and measurements. The procedures and measurements used depend upon the time period of the settlement (interim periods or final). The price is expressed as 100 minus the three-month LIBOR rate. Once this price is available, gains or losses are calculated, and the mark to market process is used to update trading accounts.

Revalue of Stock Indices at the End of Trading Day

The S&P 500 futures contract traded on the Chicago Mercantile Exchange (CME) is an appropriate example of how stock indices are revalued at the end of each trading day. The size of the contract is equal to the index value multiplied by $50 (e.g., 1470 × $50 = $73,500). The exchange determines the final index value using various procedures and measurements. The procedures and measurements used depend upon the time period of the settlement (interim periods or final). The index varies in quarters of points (for outright contracts), so the change in value of a contract is $12.50, or $50 per index full point. The calculation of gain/loss is done as follows:

S&P 500 INDEX CONTRACT		S&P 500 INDEX CONTRACT	
Standard Method		**Points Method**	
Index Value at Contract Purchase	1470.00	Index Value at Contract Purchase	1470.00
Contract Valuation	$50	Closing Value per Exchange	1464.25
Total Contract Value	$73,500.00		
		Change in Index Value	-5.75
Closing Value per Exchange	1464.25		
Contract Value at Settlement	$73,212.50	Contract Valuation	$50
GAIN/(LOSS) (mark-to-market)	-$287.50	GAIN/(LOSS) (mark-to-market)	-$287.50

EFP Process

The EFP process is used by the counterparties to a contract to determine the settlement terms privately, away from the exchange (a so-called ex-pit transaction). The terms differ from standard terms. Exchange rules typically restrict an EFP to those traders who normally deal in the underlying cash commodity, such as energy traders. The parties agree on price and delivery terms, and arrange for and accept physical delivery. The contract is formally settled by the finalization of purchase and sale of the physical commodity (buyer from seller) combined with the offsetting sale and purchase (buyer to seller) of the existing futures position.

Options Exercise, Assignment, Settlement

Assignment

Since the counterparties to a contract are unknown to each other (sales and purchases are transacted independently), it becomes the responsibility of the clearinghouse to match buyers (long position holders) with sellers (short position holders). This process is known as assignment, and is completed for each option series separately. An option series is a group of options grouped by type (call or put), expiry date, strike price, and exercise style (American or European). The assignment process of the Chicago Mercantile Exchange clearing organization (CME Clearing) involves assigning option exercises using two methods (random and pro rata), each of which is intended to be fair and equitable. The random method consists of sequential random draws for both legs of the contract from the entire pool of exercisable options of all clearing members. The long position is selected first, followed by the matching short position. The pro rata method assigns options based on the proportion of open long and short interest carried by the clearing members. For example, if clearing member *X* holds a 40% share of the total open long interest, the firm will be assigned 40% of the exercised options.

Exercise Dates

The rules of each exchange determine the dates on which options can be exercised. For example, options for ethanol futures traded on the Chicago Mercantile Exchange (CME) contain the following specifications:

- Option months: all calendar months.
- Last trading day: the last Friday preceding the first notice day of the corresponding futures contract by at least two business days.
- Exercise: American style; options may be exercised until 6:00 p.m. CT on any business day the option is traded; in the money options auto exercise at expiration.
- Unexercised ethanol futures options expire at 7:00 p.m. CT on the last day of trading.

Note that if the option is exercised European style, exercise will take place on an assigned date, which may be the expiration date of the contract or a day very close to the expiration date.

Variation of Option Premium

Option premiums typically vary based upon the amount of exercise flexibility enjoyed by traders. Since American style options can be exercised on any trading day up to the expiration date, traders are willing to pay a higher premium. In contrast, the limited flexibility afforded by European options tends to reduce the premium value.

Margin Requirements for Option with Underlying Futures Contract

The exercise of an option with an underlying futures contract results in the receipt of a long or short futures position based on the type of option (put or call, long or short). The receipt of the futures contract necessitates an immediate mark to market based on the current futures price and the option strike price. If the futures position is not immediately liquidated (closed out), it becomes a new position, necessitating the posting of an initial margin per the rules of the exchange.

Types of Orders, Customer Accounts, Price Analysis

Basic Characteristics and Uses of Orders

Order Types

The National Futures Association recognizes five basic types of orders common to most exchanges:

- market order
- limit order
- stop order
- stop limit order
- market if touched (MIT) order

<u>Market Order and Stop Order</u>

If a market order is placed, the intent of the trader is to execute the order immediately at the best possible price. A floor broker will fill the order based upon the prevailing offer, bid, or ask. When a stop order is placed, the order is not executed until either a lower or upper trigger price is reached. At that point, the order is executed at the next market price.

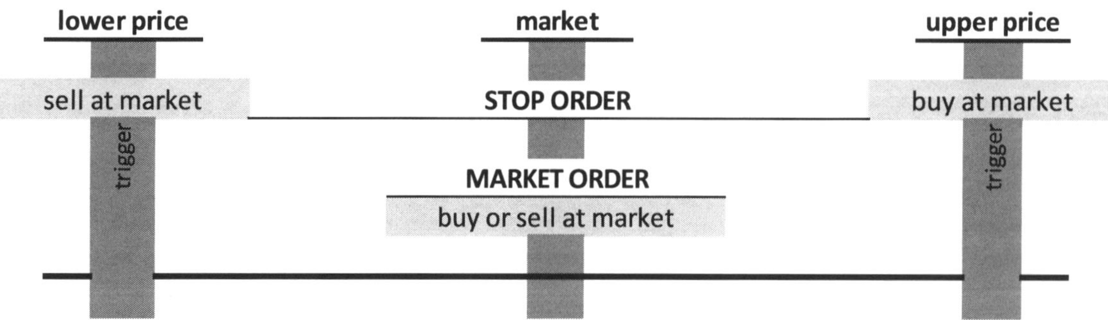

A stop order is a market order that becomes effective only after a certain trigger price is reached. In effect, a stop order converts to a market order at the trigger price, and the transaction is executed at the next market price. A sale stop order is priced lower than the present market to avoid losses due to continuing price declines. Conversely, a buy stop order is priced above market to avoid continuing price increases.

MARKET ORDER & STOP ORDER

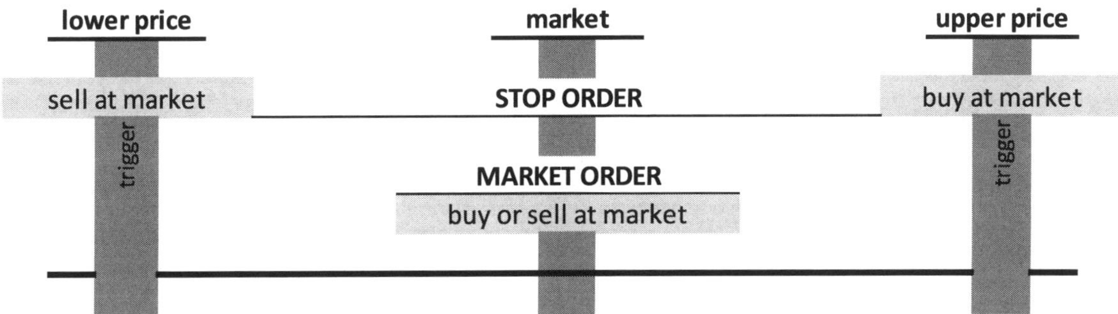

Limit Order and Stop Limit Order

A limit order is, in effect, a market order with upper and lower price parameters. The order establishes a floor or ceiling on the price at which the trade can be executed. The floor trader is expected to achieve either the limit price or better (OB). A stop limit order combines the characteristics of a trigger price (as in a stop order) and a floor or ceiling price (as in a limit order). Once the market price reaches the trigger price, the trader is instructed to buy or sell at the next most favorable price above the floor or below the ceiling.

LIMIT ORDER & STOP ORDER

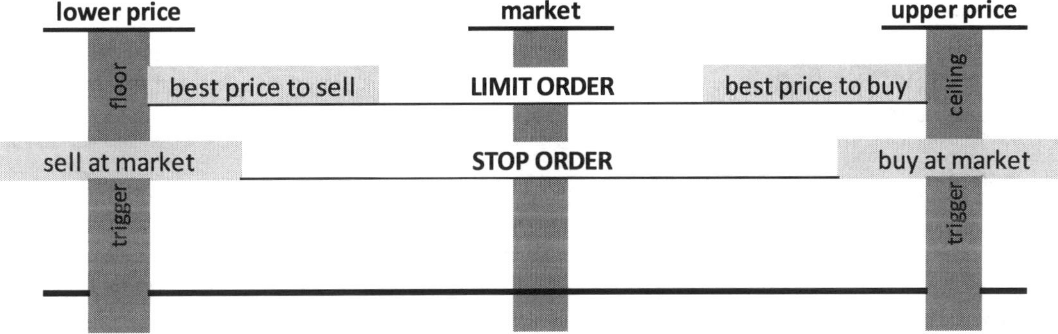

MIT Order

A market if touched order sets both a lower and an upper trigger price, as well as a subsequent floor and ceiling price. At the point that the market price reaches a trigger price (the touch point), the trigger price in effect becomes either the floor price (for a buy) or the ceiling price (for a sale). That is, the trading instructions are to execute the buy at a price not higher than the market (trigger) price. The sale is executed at a price not lower than the market price. If trading reaches a lock limit status (meaning the upper or lower limit of daily trading has been reached) either at or before the trigger price, the trade will not be executed, and will expire at the end of the trading day.

MARKET-IF-TOUCHED ORDER

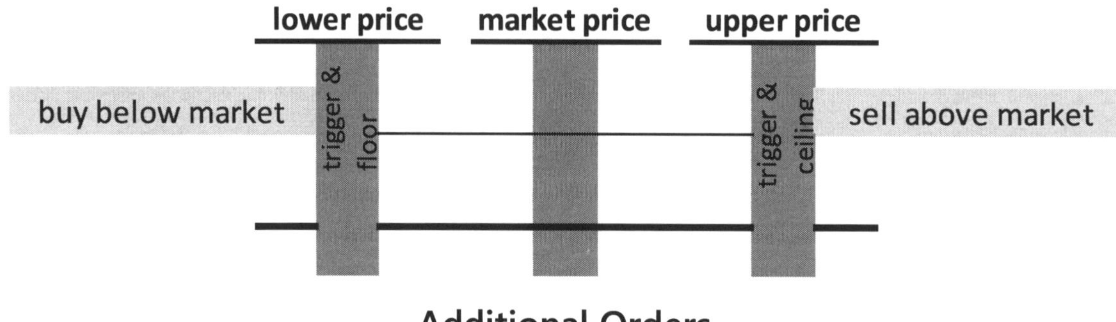

Additional Orders

Order Types

GTC Order

As its name implies, a good 'til cancelled (GTC) order remains open until a target price is reached, at which time it is immediately executed. Brokerages typically allow for a GTC order to remain open for between 30-90 days if it is not executed before 30 days elapse. A GTC order without an expiry date expires at the end of the trading day.

Fill or Kill Order

Similar to a market order, a fill or kill order is an order that is immediately executable at a currently available market price. However, any part of the order that cannot be filled must be cancelled. In practice, exchanges establish rules to guide floor brokers in their attempt to fill an order in its entirety. For example, a broker might be required to bid the open amount of the order at least three times prior to cancelling it.

MOC Order

A market on close (MOC) order instructs a floor broker to execute an order only during the official closing period of the market. The execution price will be within the range of trading during the closing period. There is no guarantee that the execution price will be the price of the actual final sale. For example, an MOC order for corn futures traded on the CME would be executed shortly before 2 p.m. on the business day prior to the 15th calendar day of the contract month.

OCO Order

A one cancels the other (OCO) order consists of two linked orders that are addressed in one set of instructions. As the name implies, if either of the two orders is executed, the other is immediately cancelled.

The two legs of the orders can consist of multiple actions, such as:

- Buy commodity *X* at market price *Y*. If not executed by the end of the day, execute MOC (for leg 1).
- Sell commodity *A* at market price *B* with a stop trigger (for leg 2).

The trader will execute either leg 1 or leg 2, but not both.

CFO

A cancel former order (CFO) is actually a combination of a cancellation of an existing order (a CXL or cancel order) and the subsequent entry of a new order. The purpose of using a single order rather than a separate cancellation order and a new order is to eliminate the possibility of the new order being executed before the cancellation order is received and executed.

OPG Order

An opening only (OPG) order is valid for execution immediately upon the opening of an exchange trading session. The order is to be immediately cancelled if it cannot be filled. It is, in effect, a time-sensitive limit order in that the trade must be executed at a limit price or better; otherwise, it is cancelled.

Electronic Trading Functionalities

The Chicago Mercantile Exchange (CME) is the largest electronic trading system, and is available 24 hours per day, five days per week. Most, but not all, of the asset classes and products that are available for open outcry can be traded electronically. Available instrument types include outright contracts on futures and options; futures spreads; and various option strategies, such as calendar spreads, straddles, and strangles. The available order types are limited to market orders with various qualifiers (which become discretionary type orders); limit orders, and stop orders. Other order qualifiers include good 'til cancelled (GTC), good 'til date (GTD), fill or kill (FOK), and fill and kill (FAK).

Valid Bid

The majority of trading that is conducted in the U.S. involves open outcry in the pit of an exchange. Buyers offer bids representing the price they are willing to pay for a commodity. Sellers, in turn, offer asks (as in asking prices) representing the price they are willing to accept for a commodity. Only the highest price offered by a buyer and the lowest price offered by a seller become valid bids. It then becomes the responsibility of the floor broker to match buyers who will meet the ask price with sellers who will meet the bid price, and vice versa.

Data Elements of a Valid Futures Order

Though the form of an order may vary among exchanges, Commodity Futures Trading Commission regulations require that all orders be time stamped at various points during the order life cycle. Orders must also include the following data elements:

- buy or sell
- quantity of contracts
- exchange, delivery month, and delivery year
- price (and any other trade conditions)
- customer account number
- period of validity (length of time the order remains open while unexecuted)

Note that unless otherwise stated, orders are assumed to be valid only for the current trading day.

Technical Price Analysis

Technical and Fundamental Market Analysis Processes

Technical analysis is based upon the study of statistical analysis, and involves looking at current and past numerical market data. A technical analyst uses statistical techniques to try to discern tendencies and trends in order to forecast future market behavior. This type of analyst often uses illustrative tools, such as charts and graphs. Fundamental analysis is based upon commodity specific information that is related to supply and demand, as well as any other factors that have an influence on the market availability of a product. A fundamental analyst would examine factors of production, such as supply and demand estimates, availability of raw materials, transportation, weather, economic events, etc. After examining these factors, the fundamental analyst would attempt to quantify a commodity's current status and probable future direction.

Data Elements Used by a Technical Analyst

Technical analysis is primarily focused on the data elements of price, volume (the number of contracts traded within a time horizon), and open interest (the "backlog" of contract commitments not yet executed).

Random Walk Theory

The random walk theory holds that securities price changes move independently such that past results cannot be used to predict future performance. Technical analysis holds that market tendencies and trends can be discerned from past performance and used to predict future movements. However, if markets are a random walk, meaning the path of change is random and thus somewhat unpredictable, technical analysis would not yield any useful results.

Charts for Trend Analysis

A line chart where the *X* axis is time and the *Y* axis is the data element being measured (price, volume, or open interest) provides a visual representation of a trend using the slope of the line. The raw data (the scatter diagram) is more useful when it is supplemented with statistical measures such as mean.

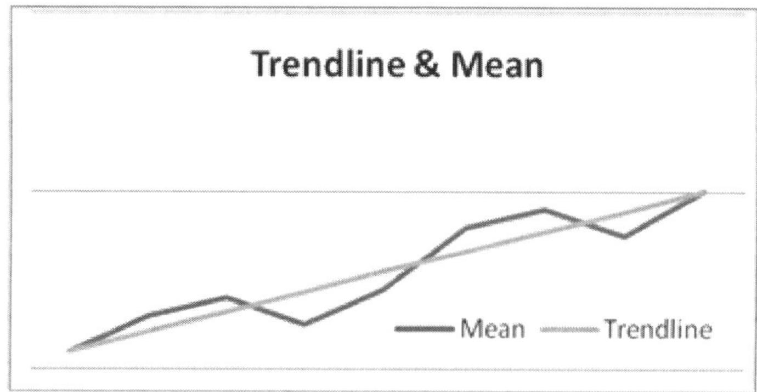

Trendline

Linear and Polynomial Functions

Useful trends are those that can be used to discern future changes. A linear function produces a linear or straight line with a constant slope. A forecast based on a linear slope essentially continues the straight line, meaning the forecasted future direction will be exactly the same as the past. However, a polynomial function is graphically represented as curvilinear, meaning the slope of the line actually changes at a changing rate. A forecast based on the slope produced from a polynomial function would anticipate this change rather than extrapolate it from a linear line.

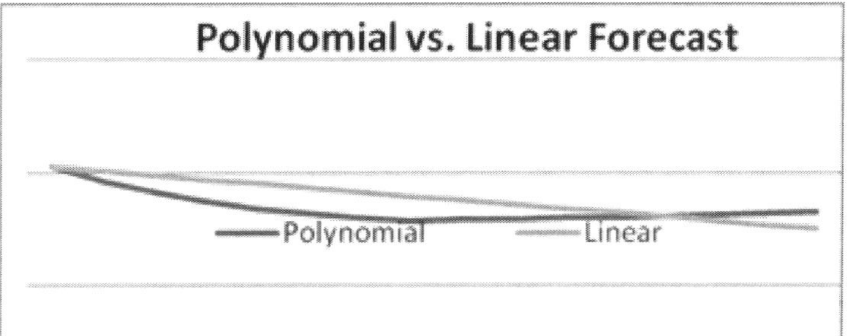

Saucer Bottom or Saucer Top

The curvilinear pattern could appear concave and resemble a saucer that is right side up (saucer bottom), or it could appear convex and resemble a saucer that is upside down (saucer top). The saucer bottom is said to indicate the level of support when the pattern begins to turn positive. In contrast, the saucer top is said to indicate the level of resistance as the pattern begins to turn negative.

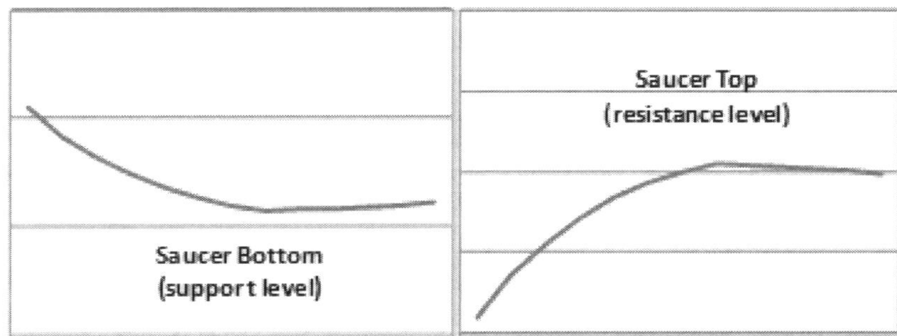

Head and Shoulders Pattern

A head and shoulders pattern is indicative of a trend reversal, which may be either positive or negative. If this trend is bearish, the pattern is characterized by successive peaks that rise to a maximum, and then fall progressively lower. An inverted head and shoulders pattern indicates a bullish trend.

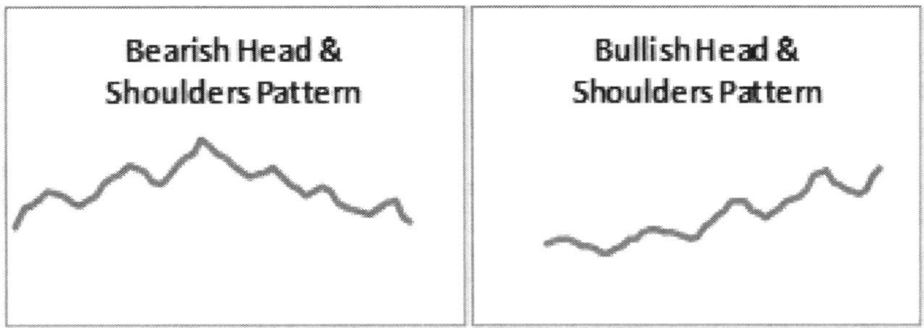

Breakout

A trend that crosses a support level (the saucer bottom) or a resistance level (the saucer top) is said to be experiencing a breakout. The latter is considered bullish, especially if the trend continues and volumes continue to rise.

Triangle

A triangle is similar to a head and shoulders pattern in that the trend takes on the form of a triangle, rising to a peak and then declining. An ascending triangle is a series of triangles, and the peak value is successively higher. At some point, usually a defined resistance level, the trend will display a breakout, which is considered bullish. A descending triangle is the opposite condition (successively lower peaks), and this trend is considered bearish.

Gap in the Price of a Security

In this instance, a gap refers to a relatively substantial difference between the closing price of a security and its opening price in the following trading period (or, in rarer circumstances, within a trading period). Such a gap can indicate a change in the underlying market fundamentals, which affect the commodity or asset underlying the contract.

Chart for Determining Trend Reversals

A chart that combines trend lines based on pricing with bars based on volume can help a trader visualize the turning points of peaks and troughs. Double tops and double bottoms are the terms used to refer to successive peaks and troughs, respectively. This pattern is significant because it is said to indicate the onset of bearish (double top) or bullish (double bottom) conditions.

Congestion

Congestion is the term used to describe the situation in which little if any change in pricing occurs over successive days. Technical analysis theory interprets a period of congestion as one in which traders are holding orders until pricing is considered more favorable. Such periods can be followed by a volume surge and a breakout in pricing. The longer the period of congestion, the greater the subsequent breakout.

A period of congestion is one in which the need of traders to offset or unwind positions is greater than the supply of traders willing to accept the counterparty position. Volume becomes stagnant, and traders are forced to pay premiums or accept discounts (depending upon the trading position) in order to execute their strategies.

Open Interest and Volume

Open interest is the measure of the number of contracts unsettled (that is, contracts that have not been delivered or liquidated) at the end of a trading period. A period of increasing open interest reflects a situation in which long positions exceed short positions, a condition known as an entering market. This type of market is considered bullish, as pricing is reinforced by new orders. Conversely, a period of decreasing open interest reflects a situation in which short positions exceed long positions, a condition known as an exiting market. This type of market is considered bearish, as more traders are leaving the market and price levels will no longer be supported.

Fundamental Price Analysis

Factors in Evaluation of a Security

A fundamental analyst is concerned with factors that are thought to influence the financial performance of the underlying entity upon which a security is based. For example, an equity analyst would examine factors such as competition, innovation, ease of market entry, capitalization, market share, and technology. Macroeconomic conditions may also be examined. These include the political environment, fiscal and tax policies, and government to government relations.

Defensive Stock

Defensive stocks are those that are characterized by consistent performance. They remain below market peaks but above market troughs. Such stocks are more resistant to changes in the economic cycle. During a period of strong growth, defensive stocks would be less favorable than growth stocks. However, in a weak economic environment, defensive stocks would be more favorable.

Factors in Evaluation of Agricultural Futures Product

An agricultural analyst would consider factors affecting crop yield and availability, such as weather, disease, pestilence, financing, transportation, and storage. Demand side factors the analyst might consider would include end user demand, substitutability, consumer trends, export opportunities, new markets, etc. Macroeconomic conditions might also be examined by the analyst. These would include government agricultural policy, the political environment, fiscal and tax policies, inflation, currency rates, and intergovernmental relations.

Inelastic Demand

When used in relation to product supply and demand, inelasticity indicates that demand will remain stable regardless of supply (and, by extension, regardless of price). An inelastic demand is generally favorable to suppliers, since the demand for their product would presumably be unaffected by any increases in price (at least in the short run).

The inelasticity of demand may indicate the level of fungibility of a product. That is, demand may remain constant regardless of price because consumers have a ready supply of acceptable substitutes. Commodities with specific grades (e.g., No. 2 yellow corn) and cross-listed stocks are examples of fungible assets.

Feed Ratio

Fair commodity prices can be figured by using various ratios. The Feed Ratio is used to describe the relationship between feeding costs and the value of livestock.

For example, a hog/corn ratio refers to the hog feeding cost as it relates to the monetary value of the hog. To derive the hog corn ratio, divide the hog price by the corn price. The hog price is based on price per hundred pounds. The corn price is based on price per bushel. When corn prices are high compared to hog prices, then it will take fewer units of corn to equal the value of 100 pounds of hog. This information will help determine what commodity should be bought or sold.

Interest Rate Analysis

Money Market and Capital Market

The distinction between the money market and the capital market is based upon the length of maturity:

- one year or less: money market
- more than one year: capital market

Money market instruments include certificates of deposit, commercial papers, banker's acceptances, and T-Bills, among others. Capital market instruments include longer-term notes and bonds for both commercial and government entities.

Yield Curve

A yield curve is a graphical representation of the return or yield of debt instruments of a like risk class. It is presented to show the returns associated with successively longer maturities. The actual measure of return is calculated as the yield to maturity. This is an iterative calculation to solve for the rate (r) at which the present value of all remaining interest payments is equal to the price paid for the bond. In effect, since the present value of the bond itself is the price paid, the yield to maturity calculation is applied to perform a reverse calculation and solve for the rate. The normal yield state for debt instruments is a higher yield for longer maturities. Therefore, a normal yield curve is polynomial and upward sloping to the right.

An inverse yield curve has the opposite shape, and indicates that shorter-term instruments have higher yields.

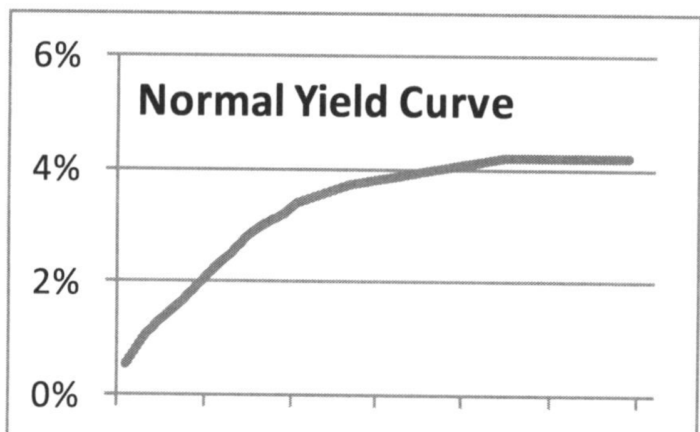

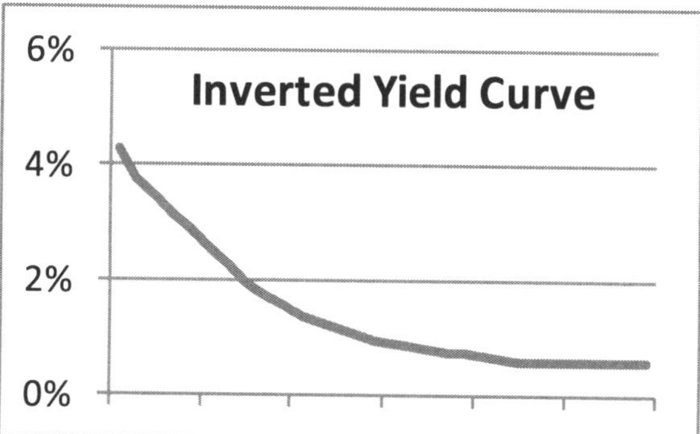

Conversion Factor Convention for Invoice Price

If a treasury bond futures contract provided for the delivery of a single bond has a face value equal to the contract value ($100,000), the formula for calculating the invoice price to be paid for the bond would be as follows:

$100,000 × Futures Settlement Price + Accrued Interest

However, the actual delivery of the bonds consists of a "basket" of various bonds, each meeting the deliverable grade criteria set by the exchange. For example, the CME lists the following criterion for long-term bonds:

- bonds with a remaining maturity of at least 15 years but less than 25 years from the first day of the delivery month

In order to equate the various bonds in the delivery basket to the single contract value, a conversion factor is applied. The invoice formula then becomes:

$100,000 × Futures Settlement Price × Conversion Factor + Accrued Interest

Structure, Pricing, and Settlement for Municipal Bond Index Futures

The Chicago Board of Trade offers a cash-settled futures contract using indices of tax-free, general obligation municipal bonds published by The Bond Buyer®. Each contract is valued at $1,000 and priced as a percentage of par (in 32nds of a point). For example, a price of 96-12 represents 96 and 12 32nds, or $96.375. The contract value would be $963.75.

Interest Cross Hedge

A cross hedge intended to manage interest rate risk is one in which the underlying security is similar to but not the same as the cash position to be protected. For example, futures contracts do not exist for corporate bonds, so traders seeking to protect such a long position must search for a product that is highly correlated, such as the Barclays U.S. Aggregate Bond Index traded on the CME.

Effect of Government Policy on Interest Rates

Monetary policy refers to the actions of a government operating through a central bank that are intended to control the money supply and, by extension, interest rates. A restrictive monetary policy is one in which interest rates are moved upward to curtail the availability of funds, while an expansionary policy moves rates lower to accommodate growth.

Fiscal policy refers to government actions that are intended to secure funds through taxation, disburse funds through a budget, and borrow funds by issuing debt instruments, all of which impact interest rates. For example, government borrowing at levels sufficient to reduce the availability of capital to private markets might cause rates to rise. Conversely, a highly conservative tax policy that increases taxpayers' disposable income might lead to lower demand for borrowing and, consequently, lower interest rates.

Basic Hedging, Basis Calculations, Hedging Futures

Short Hedging and Long Hedging

Purpose of Hedge

The purpose of a hedge is to establish a counterbalance to a risk in the cash market. A trader who enters into a hedge is typically trying to protect the value of an asset, such as a commodity or a financial instrument. Hedging transfers the risk of an adverse event to a counterparty that has an opposite risk management requirement, or to a speculator who is looking for an opportunity to make a profit.

Anticipatory Hedge

The term anticipatory hedge can refer to two opposing positions:

- A trader is long in the futures market and short in the cash market. This is known as a buying hedge. In this situation, the trader is trying to protect himself or herself against price increases.
- A trader is short in the futures market and long in the cash market. This is known as a selling hedge. In this situation, the trader is trying to protect himself or herself against price decreases.

Decision to Purchase in Cash Market or Enter into a Futures Contract

Taking delivery of a commodity can involve meeting significant logistical requirements after the actual purchase is made. Consider a cereal company that requires certain grains to use as raw material during the production process. The company can buy the grain on the cash market and take responsibility for the cost of transportation and storage, as well as any costs associated with financing and risk management (i.e. the cost of carry). Instead of accepting the logistical headaches that may be involved, the company can also choose to buy a futures contract with an expiration date that will coincide with the company's need for more grain to meet manufacturing requirements. At expiry, the company would buy the grains in the cash market and sell the futures contract. Note that in an efficient market, the price of a contract will include the cost of carry. Therefore, it would not matter whether the company purchased a cash or a futures contract, assuming prices are not expected to change in the future. The company may pay more for a futures contract, but it also saves money because the time and effort required to store the good are vastly reduced.

Selling Hedge and Buying Hedge

The example below shows two concerns that deal in heating oil. One trader has an inventory that will allow him to meet sales commitments through the following months. A different trader has sold her inventory, and will need to replenish it over the following months.

SELLING HEDGE - HEATING OIL		(1 contract = 42,000 gallons)				
CASH TRANSACTION				FUTURES TRANSACTION		
DEC	BUY 82,000 GALLONS @	$ 2.7850	$ 228,370.00	SELL 2 FEB CONTRACTS @	**$ 2.8150**	$ 236,460.00
FEB	SELL 82,000 GALLONS @	$ 2.7250	$ 223,450.00	BUY 2 FEB CONTRACTS @	$ 2.7250	$ 228,900.00
	LOSS	$ (0.0600)	$ (4,920.00)	GAIN	$ 0.0900	$ 7,560.00
EFFECTIVE PRICE:		**$ 2.8150**				

BUYING HEDGE - HEATING OIL		(1 contract = 42,000 gallons)				
CASH TRANSACTION				FUTURES TRANSACTION		
DEC	SELLS 82,000 GALLONS @	$ 2.7850	$ 228,370.00	BUY 2 FEB CONTRACTS @	**$ 2.8150**	$ 236,460.00
FEB	BUYS 82,000 GALLONS @	$ 2.7250	$ 223,450.00	SELL 2 FEB CONTRACTS @	$ 2.7250	$ 228,900.00
	GAIN	$ 0.0600	$ 4,920.00	LOSS	$ (0.0900)	$ (7,560.00)
EFFECTIVE PRICE:		**$ 2.8150**				

In the top example, the trader with inventory is concerned that the sales price will decline; the hedge is a short future. The bottom example provides details for the counterparty. This trader requires inventory, and is concerned that the sales price will advance; the hedge is a long future.

The actual price declines. The top trader avoided a steeper loss. The bottom trader incurred a higher purchase price, but because this was the futures price, this increased cost is considered acceptable.

The Basis

Basis

Basis is calculated as the difference between the cash or spot price of a commodity and an equivalent futures contract. Basis is an important concept because it reflects the pricing relationship between a cash position and a futures position. If the price of each position always reacted to changes in influential market factors (i.e. the prices were perfectly correlated), the basis would never change during the life of a futures contract. As a result, the establishment of a perfect hedge would be a simple exercise in arithmetic. The correlation between cash and futures prices is far from perfect, however, even though they are closely related. Cash markets can be immediately affected by economic and market events that are short-term or transient (such as a transportation interruption). These types of events have a lesser effect on futures. Supply or demand imbalances may move short-term prices but not long-term ones, or vice versa. Therefore, in order to establish an effective hedge, changes in basis must be considered to ascertain the appropriate composition of a futures position.

Long the Basis and Short the Basis

A selling hedge is a position consisting of a long position in the cash market and a short position in the futures market. Such a position is considered to be long the basis since any price increase (i.e. a strengthening of the basis) will benefit the long cash position.

In contrast, a buying hedge is a position consisting of a short position in the cash market and a long position in the futures market. Such a position is considered to be short the basis since any price decrease (i.e. a weakening of the basis) will benefit the short cash position. In terms of the basis (futures price – cash price), if conditions are such that the cash price rises more than the futures price (or declines less than the futures price), the basis will narrow. This is referred to as strengthening. The relative price increase accrues to the benefit of the long position. A trader with a selling or short hedge has such a long position, and is thus described as being long the basis. Conversely, when cash prices fall more than futures prices (or rise less than futures prices), the basis will widen. This is referred to as weakening. The relative price decrease accrues to the benefit of the short position. A trader with a buying or long hedge has such a short position, and is thus described as being short the basis.

Contango Market and Inverted Market

A normal market condition (contango) exists when the future price of a commodity (a futures contract) is greater than its present price (the cash price). In a normal market, the basis is negative, and usually reflects the cost of carry. An inverted market condition (backwardation) exists when the future price of a commodity is less than the cash market price of the commodity. In an inverted market, the basis is positive, and this may be the result of near-term supply shortages.

Basis Risk

A fundamental concept that underlies an effective hedging strategy is that the basis between a cash and a futures contract will remain relatively unchanged. Therefore, pricing fluctuations in the cash market will be closely correlated with fluctuations in the futures market, enabling a net zero offset from the eventual liquidation. Basis risk represents the probability that the correlation described above will be weaker than anticipated. If this occurs, cash and futures prices will diverge, leading to an unfavorable result at the time of liquidation. An agricultural producer with product to sell has a long position in the cash market. The producer has the option of selling in the cash market or selling a contract for future delivery. The key consideration for the producer is which opportunity will result in a more favorable selling price. Basis will have an impact on whether the futures contract ends up being underpriced as a result of strengthening or favorably priced as a result of weakening. Either condition will play a role in the producer's decision.

Influences on Basis of Product

In addition to transportation costs and variations in deliverable grades, there are a number of other factors that can have an influence on the basis of a product:

- supply and demand disruptions
- substitution (availability of)

- local geography
- storage and handling

Events or circumstances that can affect either cash markets or futures markets (but not both) can cause the basis to narrow (strengthen) or widen (weaken).

Price of Financial Futures

The primary (and often only) component of the basis for financial futures (and most other cash-settled futures) is the cost of funds, which is expressed as interest. A change in basis is a function of changes in expected interest rates. In a period of rising interest rates, the basis would become positive, reflecting the inverse relationship between rates and prices. Conversely, the basis would become negative during a period of declining interest rates.

Benefits of Hedges for Holders of Financial Assets

A hedge can protect the value of a portfolio by establishing a ceiling or floor beyond which the gain on a futures contract will offset the loss due to adverse interest rates. For example, rising long-term interest rates would cause the value of a portfolio of treasury notes to decline because of the inverse relationship between interest rates and bond prices. The holder of the notes could sell treasury note futures, which would serve as an offset to the decline in the value of the note portfolio.

Repurchase Agreement

A repurchase agreement is essentially a loan between parties that is secured by the value of a financial instrument, such as an equity security. The buying party agrees to accept the underlying instrument for a period of time. The selling party agrees to buy it back (repurchase it) at a specified price at the end of the agreed upon time period. The difference between the selling price and the repurchase price is the implied rate of interest, which is known as the repurchase rate.

Hedging Calculations

Declining and Advancing Prices

A short hedge position offers protection from a decline in pricing because the value of the futures contract will increase if prices drop, offsetting the decline in value of the cash position. However, a short hedger will incur losses if prices advance. Conversely, a long hedge position offers protection from an increase in pricing because the value of the futures contract will increase if prices rise, offsetting the higher purchase price associated with the cash position. However, a long hedger will incur losses if prices decline.

Net Result of Hedge and Net Price for Short and Long Positions

<u>During Declining Prices</u>

Using the following recent quote information, calculate the net result of the hedge and the net price received for both the short and long positions during a period of declining prices:

SOYBEAN QUOTE (CBOT)				
CURRENT DATE: JAN 2013				
FUTURES DATE: JUL 2013				
PRICING UNIT: CENTS PER BUSHEL				
		UNIT PRICE		
		SHORT	**LONG**	
	sell	**HEDGE**	**HEDGE**	*buy*
FUTURES CONTRACT SIZE IN BUSHELS		5,000	5,000	
QUANTITY OF BUSHELS TO HEDGE		300,000	300,000	
NUMBER OF CONTRACTS REQUIRED		60	60	
CASH PRICE (AVAILABLE FORWARD CONTRACT)		1,424	1,424	
FUTURES CONTRACT PRICE		1,404	1,404	
ACTUAL PRICE IN MONTH OF SALE/PURCHASE		1,390	1,390	
ACTUAL FUTURES CLOSE-OUT PRICE		1,395	1,395	

Calculation of results:

		UNIT PRICE				**CONTRACT VALUE**		
		SHORT	**LONG**			**SHORT**	**LONG**	
	sell	**HEDGE**	**HEDGE**	*buy*	*sell*	**HEDGE**	**HEDGE**	*buy*
CASH SETTLEMENT RESULT:								
ACTUAL PRICE IN MONTH OF SALE/PURCHASE		1,390	1,390			$ 4,170,000	$ 4,170,000	
FUTURES CONTRACT SETTLEMENT RESULT:								
FUTURES CONTRACT PRICE		1,404	1,404			$ 4,212,000	$ 4,212,000	
ACTUAL FUTURES CLOSE-OUT PRICE (IN DELIVERY MONTH)		1,395	1,395			$ 4,185,000	$ 4,185,000	
GAIN / (LOSS)		9	(9)			$ 27,000	$ (27,000)	
						$ 4,197,000	$ 4,197,000	
NET UNIT PRICE PER BUSHEL		1,399	1,399			$ 13.99	$ 13.99	

The short hedger sold in the cash market at 1390, but offset the lower price with a gain of 9 on the futures contract. The effective selling price was 1399 cents per bushel, a result that was more favorable than 1390. The short hedger benefitted from the decline in price. The long hedger purchased in the cash market for 1390, but experienced a loss of 9 on the futures contract. The effective purchase price was 1399 cents per bushel. The long hedger suffered from the decline in price.

During Advancing Prices

Using the following recent quote information, calculate the net result of the hedge and the net price received for both the short and long positions during a period of advancing prices:

SOYBEAN QUOTE (CBOT)			
CURRENT DATE: JAN 2013			
FUTURES DATE: JUL 2013			
PRICING UNIT: CENTS PER BUSHEL			
		UNIT PRICE	
	sell	SHORT HEDGE	LONG HEDGE	buy
FUTURES CONTRACT SIZE IN BUSHELS		5,000	5,000	
QUANTITY OF BUSHELS TO HEDGE		300,000	300,000	
NUMBER OF CONTRACTS REQUIRED		60	60	
CASH PRICE (AVAILABLE FORWARD CONTRACT)		1,424	1,424	
FUTURES CONTRACT PRICE		1,404	1,404	
ACTUAL PRICE IN MONTH OF SALE/PURCHASE		1,452	1,452	
ACTUAL FUTURES CLOSE-OUT PRICE		1,457	1,457	

Calculation of results:

		UNIT PRICE				CONTRACT VALUE		
	sell	SHORT HEDGE	LONG HEDGE	buy	sell	SHORT HEDGE	LONG HEDGE	buy
CASH SETTLEMENT RESULT:								
ACTUAL PRICE IN MONTH OF SALE/PURCHASE		1,452	1,452			$ 4,356,000	$ 4,356,000	
FUTURES CONTRACT SETTLEMENT RESULT:								
FUTURES CONTRACT PRICE		1,404	1,404			$ 4,212,000	$ 4,212,000	
ACTUAL FUTURES CLOSE-OUT PRICE (IN DELIVERY MONTH)		1,457	1,457			$ 4,371,000	$ 4,371,000	
GAIN / (LOSS)		(53)	53			$ (159,000)	$ 159,000	
						$ 4,197,000	$ 4,197,000	
NET UNIT PRICE PER BUSHEL		1,399	1,399			$ 13.99	$ 13.99	

The short hedger sold at 1452, but experienced a loss of 53 on the futures contract. The effective selling price was 1399. The short hedger suffered from the increase in price.

The long hedger purchased at 1452, but offset the higher price with a gain of 53 on the futures contract. The effective purchase price was 1399. The long hedger benefitted from the increase in price.

Perfect Hedge

A perfect hedge assumes that a futures contract can be executed and that an offset with the exact same quantity and price as the underlying cash position will be available. In other words, a perfect hedge assumes that changes in one position (cash or futures) will be exactly offset by equal but opposite changes in the other. Hedges are rarely perfect since futures contracts use standardized terms. For example, a contract for ethanol is equal to 29,000 gallons (one rail car). Should the required hedge not be a multiple of 29,000, the hedge will not be perfect. Likewise, a contract may not be available at the price required due to various factors, such as a trading halt at locked limit or another type of market interruption.

Short and Long Hedge Calculation Examples

Soybeans

COMMODITY: AGRICULTURAL (SOYBEANS)				
CURRENT DATE: JAN 2013				
FUTURES DATE: JUL 2013				
PRICING UNIT: CENTS PER BUSHEL				
		UNIT PRICE		
		SHORT HEDGE (protection against declining prices)	LONG HEDGE (protection against advancing prices)	
FUTURES CONTRACT SIZE IN BUSHELS		5,000	5,000	
QUANTITY OF BUSHELS TO HEDGE		300,000	300,000	
NUMBER OF CONTRACTS REQUIRED		60	60	
CASH PRICE (Based on available Jan. forward contract)		1,424	1,424	
HEDGE ASSUMPTION:		Prices will decline reducing future selling price	Prices will advance increasing future purchase price	
AVAILABLE HEDGE: FUTURES CONTRACT AT A PRICE OF.....	*sell*	1,440	1,440	*buy*
CASH SETTLEMENT RESULT:				
ACTUAL CASH PRICE IN JULY		1,360	1,470	
FUTURES CONTRACT SETTLEMENT RESULT:				
FUTURES CONTRACT PRICE		1,440	1,440	
ACTUAL FUTURES CLOSE-OUT PRICE (IN DELIVERY MONTH)		1,360	1,470	
NET BENEFIT FROM HEDGE		80	30	
NET UNIT PRICE PER BUSHEL		1,440	1,440	
Benefit to the trader:		*sell at 1440 rather than 1360*	*buy at 1440 rather than 1470*	

Livestock (Live Cattle)

COMMODITY: LIVESTOCK (LIVE CATTLE)				
CURRENT DATE: FEB 2013				
FUTURES DATE: AUG 2013				
PRICING UNIT: CENTS PER POUND				
		UNIT PRICE		
		SHORT HEDGE (protection against declining prices)	**LONG HEDGE** (protection against advancing prices)	
FUTURES CONTRACT SIZE IN POUNDS		40,000	40,000	
POUNDS TO HEDGE		600,000	600,000	
NUMBER OF CONTRACTS REQUIRED		15	15	
CASH PRICE (Based on available Feb. forward contract)		124.950	124.950	
HEDGE ASSUMPTION:		Prices will decline reducing future selling price	Prices will advance increasing future purchase price	
AVAILABLE HEDGE: FUTURES CONTRACT AT A PRICE OF.....	*sell*	129.525	129.525	*buy*
CASH SETTLEMENT RESULT:				
ACTUAL CASH PRICE IN AUGUST		120.950	136.450	
FUTURES CONTRACT SETTLEMENT RESULT:				
FUTURES CONTRACT PRICE		129.525	129.525	
ACTUAL FUTURES CLOSE-OUT PRICE (IN DELIVERY MONTH)		120.950	136.450	
NET BENEFIT FROM HEDGE		8.575	6.925	
NET UNIT PRICE PER POUND		129.525	129.525	
Benefit to the trader:		***sell at 129.525 rather than 120.950***	***buy at 129.525 rather than 136.450***	

Foodstuffs (Cheese)

COMMODITY: FOODSTUFFS (CHEESE - cash settled)				
CURRENT DATE: FEB 2013				
FUTURES DATE: AUG 2013				
PRICING UNIT: CENTS PER POUND				
		UNIT PRICE		
		SHORT HEDGE (protection against declining prices)	**LONG HEDGE** (protection against advancing prices)	
FUTURES CONTRACT SIZE IN POUNDS		20,000	20,000	
POUNDS TO HEDGE		600,000	600,000	
NUMBER OF CONTRACTS REQUIRED		30	30	
CASH PRICE (Based on available Feb. forward contract)		1.700	1.700	
HEDGE ASSUMPTION:		Prices will decline reducing future selling price	Prices will advance increasing future purchase price	
AVAILABLE HEDGE: FUTURES CONTRACT AT A PRICE OF.....	*sell*	1.860	1.860	*buy*
CASH SETTLEMENT RESULT:				
ACTUAL CASH PRICE IN AUGUST		1.420	1.970	
FUTURES CONTRACT SETTLEMENT RESULT:				
FUTURES CONTRACT PRICE		1.860	1.860	
ACTUAL FUTURES CLOSE-OUT PRICE (IN DELIVERY MONTH)		1.420	1.970	
NET BENEFIT FROM HEDGE		0.440	0.110	
NET UNIT PRICE PER POUND		1.860	1.860	
Benefit to the trader:		***sell at 1.860 rather than 1.420***	***buy at 1.860 rather than 1.970***	

Metals (Silver)

COMMODITY: METALS (SILVER)			
CURRENT DATE: JAN 2013			
FUTURES DATE: JUL 2013			
PRICING UNIT: CENTS PER TROY OUNCE			
		UNIT PRICE		
		SHORT HEDGE (protection against declining prices)	LONG HEDGE (protection against advancing prices)	
FUTURES CONTRACT SIZE IN TROY OUNCES		5,000	5,000	
OUNCES TO HEDGE		600,000	600,000	
NUMBER OF CONTRACTS REQUIRED		120	120	
CASH PRICE (Based on available Jan. forward contract)		$ 32.147	$ 32.147	
HEDGE ASSUMPTION:		Prices will decline reducing future selling price	Prices will advance increasing future purchase price	
AVAILABLE HEDGE: FUTURES CONTRACT AT A PRICE OF.....	*sell*	$ 32.287	$ 32.287	*buy*
CASH SETTLEMENT RESULT:				
ACTUAL CASH PRICE IN JULY		$ 29.442	$ 33.988	
FUTURES CONTRACT SETTLEMENT RESULT:				
FUTURES CONTRACT PRICE		$ 32.287	$ 32.287	
ACTUAL FUTURES CLOSE-OUT PRICE (IN DELIVERY MONTH)		$ 29.442	$ 33.988	
NET BENEFIT FROM HEDGE		$ 2.845	$ 1.701	
NET UNIT PRICE PER TROY OUNCE		$ 32.287	$ 32.287	
Benefit to the trader:		***sell at 32.287 rather than 29.442***	***buy at 32.287 rather than 33.988***	

Energy (Ethanol)

COMMODITY: ENERGY (ETHANOL)				
CURRENT DATE: FEB 2013				
FUTURES DATE: AUG 2013				
PRICING UNIT: DOLLARS AND CENTS PER GALLON				
		UNIT PRICE		
		SHORT HEDGE (protection against declining prices)	LONG HEDGE (protection against advancing prices)	
FUTURES CONTRACT SIZE IN GALLONS		29,000	29,000	
GALLONS TO HEDGE		600,000	600,000	
NUMBER OF CONTRACTS REQUIRED		21	21	
CASH PRICE (Based on available Feb. forward contract)		$ 2.375	$ 2.375	
HEDGE ASSUMPTION:		Prices will decline reducing future selling price	Prices will advance increasing future purchase price	
AVAILABLE HEDGE: FUTURES CONTRACT AT A PRICE OF.....	*sell*	$ 2.198	$ 2.198	*buy*
CASH SETTLEMENT RESULT:				
ACTUAL CASH PRICE IN AUGUST		$ 2.056	$ 2.299	
FUTURES CONTRACT SETTLEMENT RESULT:				
FUTURES CONTRACT PRICE		$ 2.198	$ 2.198	
ACTUAL FUTURES CLOSE-OUT PRICE (IN DELIVERY MONTH)		$ 2.056	$ 2.299	
NET BENEFIT FROM HEDGE		$ 0.142	$ 0.101	
NET UNIT PRICE PER GALLON		$ 2.198	$ 2.198	
Benefit to the trader:		***sell at 2.198 rather than 2.056***	***buy at 2.198 rather than 2.299***	

Lumber (Softwood Pulp)

COMMODITY: LUMBER (RANDOM LENGTH)				
CURRENT DATE: MAR 2013				
FUTURES DATE: SEP 2013				
PRICING UNIT: DOLLARS PER THOUSAND BOARD FEET				
		UNIT PRICE		
		SHORT HEDGE (protection against declining prices)	**LONG HEDGE** (protection against advancing prices)	
FUTURES CONTRACT SIZE IN BOARD FEET		110,000	110,000	
BOARD FEET TO HEDGE		600,000	600,000	
NUMBER OF CONTRACTS REQUIRED		5	5	
CASH PRICE (Based on available Mar. forward contract)		362.30	362.30	
HEDGE ASSUMPTION:		Prices will decline reducing future selling price	Prices will advance increasing future purchase price	
AVAILABLE HEDGE: FUTURES CONTRACT AT A PRICE OF.....	*sell*	349.70	349.70	*buy*
CASH SETTLEMENT RESULT:				
ACTUAL CASH PRICE IN SEPTEMBER		332.60	358.10	
FUTURES CONTRACT SETTLEMENT RESULT:				
FUTURES CONTRACT PRICE		349.70	349.70	
ACTUAL FUTURES CLOSE-OUT PRICE (IN DELIVERY MONTH)		332.60	358.10	
NET BENEFIT FROM HEDGE		17.10	8.40	
NET UNIT PRICE PER THOUSAND BOARD FT		349.70	349.70	
Benefit to the trader:		***sell at 349.70 rather than 332.60***	***buy at 349.70 rather than 358.10***	

T-Bonds (30 Year)

COMMODITY: U.S. TREASURY BONDS						
CURRENT DATE: MAR 2013						
FUTURES DATE: SEP 2013						
PRICING UNIT: PERCENTAGE OF PAR PLUS 32nds						
ASSUMED COUPON RATE: 6.0%						
ASSUMED YEARS TO MATURITY: 15.0		SHORT HEDGE		LONG HEDGE		
		UNIT PRICE	RATE OF INTEREST *	UNIT PRICE	RATE OF INTEREST *	
FUTURES CONTRACT SIZE IN USD		$ 100,000		$ 100,000		
CASH PRICE (Based on available Mar. forward contract)		146.27	*2.051%*	146.27	*2.051%*	
HEDGE ASSUMPTION:		Rates will rise reducing value of current holdings		Rates will decline; lock-in best rate		
AVAILABLE HEDGE: FUTURES CONTRACT AT A PRICE OF.....	*sell*	144.11	*2.082%*	144.11	*2.082%*	*buy*
CASH SETTLEMENT RESULT:						
ACTUAL PRICE IN SEPTEMBER		142.08	*2.111%*	145.21	*2.066%*	
FUTURES CONTRACT SETTLEMENT RESULT:						
FUTURES CONTRACT PRICE		144.11		144.11		
ACTUAL FUTURES CLOSE-OUT PRICE (IN DELIVERY MONTH)		142.08		145.21		
NET BENEFIT FROM HEDGE		2.03	2 3/32	1.10	1 10/32	
		$ 2,093.75		$ 1,312.50		
Benefit to the trader:		***contract gain offset loss to current holdings***		***contract gain offset reduced return on purchase***		

T-Notes (5 Year)

COMMODITY: U.S. TREASURY NOTES (5 YEAR)						
CURRENT DATE: MAR 2013						
FUTURES DATE: SEP 2013						
PRICING UNIT: PERCENTAGE OF PAR PLUS 32nds & QUARTERS OF 32nds						
ASSUMED COUPON RATE: 6.0%						
ASSUMED YEARS TO MATURITY: 2.5		**SHORT HEDGE**		**LONG HEDGE**		
		UNIT PRICE	**RATE OF INTEREST ***	**UNIT PRICE**	**RATE OF INTEREST ***	
FUTURES CONTRACT SIZE IN USD		$ 100,000		$ 100,000		
CASH PRICE (Based on available Mar. forward contract)		124.072	*2.418%*	124.072	*2.418%*	
HEDGE ASSUMPTION:		Rates will rise reducing value of current holdings		Rates will decline; lock-in best rate		
AVAILABLE HEDGE: FUTURES CONTRACT AT A PRICE OF.....	*sell*	123.054	*2.438%*	123.054	*2.438%*	*buy*
CASH SETTLEMENT RESULT:						
ACTUAL PRICE IN SEPTEMBER		121.042	*2.478%*	124.172	*2.416%*	
FUTURES CONTRACT SETTLEMENT RESULT:						
FUTURES CONTRACT PRICE		123.054		123.054		
ACTUAL FUTURES CLOSE-OUT PRICE (IN DELIVERY MONTH)		121.042		124.172		
NET BENEFIT FROM HEDGE		2.012	2 1.25/32	1.118	1 11.75/32	
		$ 2,039.06		$ 1,367.19		
Benefit to the trader:		***contract gain offset loss to current holdings***		***contract gain offset reduced return on purchase***		

T-Bills (13 Week)

COMMODITY: U.S. TREASURY BILLS (13 WEEK)
CURRENT DATE: MAR 2013
FUTURES DATE: SEP 2013
PRICING UNIT: 100 MINUS ANNUALIZED DISCOUNT RATE

		SHORT HEDGE		LONG HEDGE		
		UNIT PRICE	**RATE OF INTEREST ***	**UNIT PRICE**	**RATE OF INTEREST ***	
FUTURES CONTRACT SIZE IN USD		$ 1,000,000		$ 1,000,000		
CASH PRICE (Based on available Mar. forward contract)		99.270	*0.730%*	99.270	*0.730%*	
HEDGE ASSUMPTION:		Rates will rise reducing value of current holdings		Rates will decline; lock-in best rate		
AVAILABLE HEDGE: FUTURES CONTRACT AT A PRICE OF.....	*sell*	99.255	*0.745%*	99.255	*0.745%*	*buy*
CASH SETTLEMENT RESULT:						
ACTUAL PRICE IN SEPTEMBER		99.245	*0.755%* increase	99.285	*0.715%* decrease	
FUTURES CONTRACT SETTLEMENT RESULT:						
FUTURES CONTRACT PRICE		99.255		99.255		
ACTUAL FUTURES CLOSE-OUT PRICE (IN DELIVERY MONTH)		99.245		99.285		
NET BENEFIT FROM HEDGE		0.010		0.030		
		$ 25.00		$ 75.00		
Benefit to the trader:		***contract gain offset loss to current holdings***		***contract gain offset reduced return on purchase***		

Eurodollars

COMMODITY: EURODOLLARS						
CURRENT DATE: MAR 2013						
FUTURES DATE: SEP 2013						
PRICING UNIT: 100 MINUS ANNUALIZED DISCOUNT RATE						
		SHORT HEDGE		LONG HEDGE		
		UNIT PRICE	RATE OF INTEREST *	UNIT PRICE	RATE OF INTEREST *	
FUTURES CONTRACT SIZE IN USD		$ 1,000,000		$ 1,000,000		
CASH PRICE (Based on available Mar. forward contract)		99.695	*0.305%*	99.695	*0.305%*	
HEDGE ASSUMPTION:		Rates will rise reducing value of current holdings		Rates will decline; lock-in best rate		
AVAILABLE HEDGE: FUTURES CONTRACT AT A PRICE OF.....	*sell*	99.690	*0.310%*	99.690	*0.310%*	*buy*
CASH SETTLEMENT RESULT:						
ACTUAL PRICE IN SEPTEMBER		99.660	*0.340%* increase	99.699	*0.301%* decrease	
FUTURES CONTRACT SETTLEMENT RESULT:						
FUTURES CONTRACT PRICE		99.690		99.690		
ACTUAL FUTURES CLOSE-OUT PRICE (IN DELIVERY MONTH)		99.660		99.699		
NET BENEFIT FROM HEDGE		0.030		0.009		
		$ 75.00		$ 22.50		
Benefit to the trader:		***contract gain offset loss to current holdings***		***contract gain offset reduced return on purchase***		

Municipals

COMMODITY: MUNICIPALS (BOND BUYER INDEX)						
CURRENT DATE: MAR 2010						
FUTURES DATE: SEP 2010						
PRICING UNIT: PERCENTAGE OF PAR PLUS 32nds						
ASSUMED COUPON RATE: 4.0%						
		SHORT HEDGE		**LONG HEDGE**		
		UNIT PRICE	**RATE OF INTEREST ***	**UNIT PRICE**	**RATE OF INTEREST ***	
FUTURES CONTRACT SIZE IN USD		$ 100,000		$ 100,000		
CASH PRICE (Based on available Mar. forward contract)		115.25	*1.735%*	115.25	*1.735%*	
HEDGE ASSUMPTION:		Rates will rise reducing value of current holdings		Rates will decline; lock-in best rate		
AVAILABLE HEDGE: FUTURES CONTRACT AT A PRICE OF.....	*sell*	117.10	*1.708%*	117.10	*1.708%*	*buy*
CASH SETTLEMENT RESULT:						
ACTUAL PRICE IN SEPTEMBER		114.04	*1.754%*	118.28	*1.691%*	
FUTURES CONTRACT SETTLEMENT RESULT:						
FUTURES CONTRACT PRICE		117.10		117.10		
ACTUAL FUTURES CLOSE-OUT PRICE (IN DELIVERY MONTH)		114.04		118.28		
NET BENEFIT FROM HEDGE		3.06	3 6/32	1.18	1 18/32	
		$ 3,187.50		$ 1,562.50		
Benefit to the trader:		***contract gain offset loss to current holdings***		***contract gain offset reduced return on purchase***		

Currencies (JPY/USD)

COMMODITY: CURRENCY RATES JPY : USD							
CURRENT DATE: MAR 2013							
FUTURES DATE: SEP 2013							
PRICING UNIT: .10 INDEX POINTS X $25							
CONTRACT VALUE: INDEX PRICE X $250							
		SHORT HEDGE		LONG HEDGE			
		UNIT PRICE	1 USD	UNIT PRICE	1 USD		
	FUTURES CONTRACT SIZE IN JPY		¥12,500,000		¥12,500,000		
	CASH PRICE (Based on available Mar. forward contract)		$ 0.0112740	88.70	$ 0.0112740	88.70	
	HEDGE ASSUMPTION:		Yen will weaken reducing value of yen denominated assets		Yen will strengthen increasing value of yen denominated liabilities		
	AVAILABLE HEDGE: FUTURES CONTRACT AT A PRICE OF.....	*sell*	$ 0.0112830	88.63	$ 0.0112830	88.63	*buy*
CASH SETTLEMENT RESULT:							
	ACTUAL PRICE IN SEPTEMBER		$ 0.0110020	90.89	$ 0.0115210	86.80	
FUTURES CONTRACT SETTLEMENT RESULT:							
	FUTURES CONTRACT PRICE		$ 0.0112830	88.63	$ 0.01128300	88.63	
	ACTUAL FUTURES CLOSE-OUT PRICE (IN DELIVERY MONTH)		$ 0.0110020	90.89	$ 0.01152100	86.80	
	NET BENEFIT FROM HEDGE		$ 0.0002810		$ 0.0002380		
			$ 3,512.50		$ 2,975.00		
	Benefit to the trader:		***contract gain offset loss on yen assets***		***contract gain offset loss on yen liabilities***		

Stock Indices (S&P 500)

COMMODITY: STOCK INDEX S&P 500				
CURRENT DATE: MAR 2013				
FUTURES DATE: SEP 2013				
PRICING UNIT: .10 INDEX POINTS X $25				
CONTRACT VALUE: INDEX PRICE X $250				
		SHORT HEDGE	**LONG HEDGE**	
		UNIT PRICE	**UNIT PRICE**	
FUTURES CONTRACT SIZE IN USD		$ 372,350	$ 372,350	
CASH PRICE (Based on available Mar. forward contract)		1,489.40	1,489.40	
HEDGE ASSUMPTION:		Index will fall reducing value of current holdings	Index will rise increasing future purchase prices	
AVAILABLE HEDGE: FUTURES CONTRACT AT A PRICE OF.....	*sell*	1,475.80	1,475.80	*buy*
CASH SETTLEMENT RESULT:				
ACTUAL PRICE IN SEPTEMBER		1,442.50	1,502.25	
FUTURES CONTRACT SETTLEMENT RESULT:				
FUTURES CONTRACT PRICE		1,475.80	1,475.80	
ACTUAL FUTURES CLOSE-OUT PRICE (IN DELIVERY MONTH)		1,442.50	1,502.25	
NET BENEFIT FROM HEDGE		33.30	26.45	
		$ 8,325.00	$ 6,612.50	
Benefit to the trader:		***contract gain offset loss to current holdings***	***contract gain offset higher price on purchase***	

Spreading

Spread Trading

Spread Trade

A spread is a futures contract that includes two offsetting market positions (long and short) called legs that are entered as a single order. The goal of a spread is to benefit from the relationship between the two positions, rather than to benefit from each position separately. The underlying objective is to reduce the level of risk beyond the reduction that is possible with two separate positions. For example, an entity that creates a finished product from commodity raw materials may need to take a long position for the commodities to lock in a favorable price. And, in order to hedge against a future price decline for the finished product, a short position would be required. Both of these positions can be entered as a single spread order.

Order Entry

Most exchanges allow spreads to be entered as single orders rather than as multiple separate orders. A single order containing both legs of the trade is preferable to separate orders because the order entry and liquidation process is simplified, margin requirements are significantly lower (because of the reduction in volatility that results from offsetting short and long positions), and each leg works in relation to the other (via changes in basis).

Margin Requirements for Hedgers and Speculators

Margins are known as performance bonds, and this term reflects their essential purpose. They are a risk management tool intended to guarantee contract performance in the event that adverse circumstances arise. Since hedgers maintain an underlying cash position, they have a greater ability to meet their obligations than speculators, whose cash positions are said to be "naked." Spread margins are calculated using individual outright margins as a basis. These margins are adjusted to reflect the reduced risk of an order with offsetting (short and long) positions. Since outright margins are higher for speculators than they are for hedgers, the resulting spread margins are higher as well.

The following is a simple example:

SOYBEAN MEAL CALENDAR SPREAD	Outright Margin	Contract Ratio	Total Margin	Spread Credit	Spread Margin
1 LONG SOYBEAN MEAL	$ 2,000	1	$ 2,000	87.5%	$ 250
1 SHORT SOYBEAN MEAL	$ 2,000	1	$ 2,000	87.5%	$ 250
			$ 4,000		**$ 500**

Value of Spread Order in Normal Market and Inverted Market

In a normal market, the basis of a spread order will be negative; the longer-term futures price will be higher than the shorter-term one. The expectation of the trader is that the basis will narrow as the contract approaches expiration. In this case, a trader would buy the near-term contract (with the expectation of modestly higher prices) and sell the longer-term contract (with the expectation of lower prices). In an inverted market, the near-term contract price will be higher than the longer-term one, and the basis will be positive. The expectation of the trader is that the basis will widen as price normalizes. The trader would sell the near-term contract (with the expectation of lower prices) and buy the longer-term contract (with the expectation of higher prices).

Commodities Used in Product Spread

The intent of a product spread is to establish opposite positions in a raw material and a derived product. The two primary types of product spreads are as follows:

- crush spread – raw material: soybeans; derived products: soybean oil, soybean meal
- crack spread – raw material: crude oil; derived products: gasoline, heating oil

The spread consists of a long position in the raw material and a short position in the derived products. A reverse spread consists of a long position in the derived products and a short position in the raw materials. The position is created by comparing the derived product yield to the amount of raw materials required to produce that yield. For example, if 10,000 bushels of soybeans yield 5,000 gallons of oil and 3,000 pounds of meal, the contract values will be 10:5:3.

Common Types of Spreads

Bull Spread and Bear Spread

A bull spread and a bear spread are designed to yield a profit in opposing price scenarios. A bull spread consists of a long position in the near futures contract and a short position in the outer futures contract. The trader will benefit when the basis narrows (i.e. the price of the near futures contract increases and/or the price of the outer futures contract decreases). A bear spread has the same structure as a bull spread, but the short and long positions are reversed. A bear spread consists of a short position in the near futures contract and a long position in the outer futures contract. The trader will benefit when the basis widens (i.e. the price of the near futures contract decreases and/or the price of the outer futures contract increases).

Price Expectations for Bull Spread in Normal and Inverted Markets

A trader who enters into a bull spread in a normal market seeks to benefit from a narrowing of the basis. This occurs when the price of the short leg (the outer contract) declines and/or the price of the long leg (the near contract) increases.

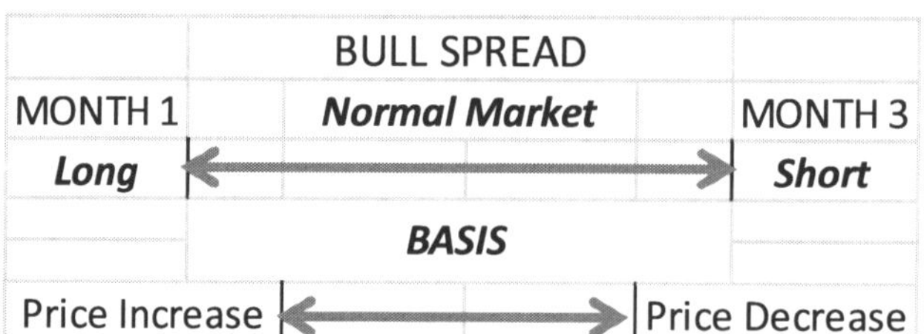

In an inverted market, the bull spread would need to have an opposite structure compared to the one used in a normal market. The near contract would be the short leg, and the outer contract would be the long leg. The trader would seek to benefit from a widening basis (i.e. increasing prices for the outer contract and/or decreasing prices for the near contract).

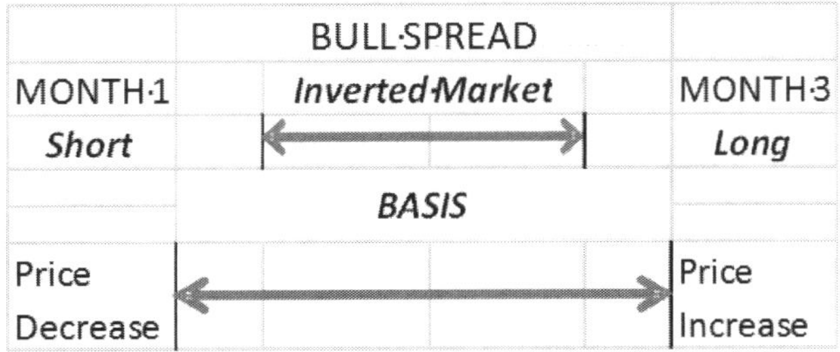

Price Expectations for Bear Spread in Normal and Inverted Markets

A trader who enters into a bear spread in an inverted market seeks to benefit from a narrowing of the basis. This occurs when the price of the short leg (the outer contract) declines and/or the price of the long leg (the near contract) increases.

In a normal market, the bear spread would need to have an opposite structure compared to the one used in an inverted market. The near contract would be the short leg, and the outer contract would be the long leg. The trader would seek to benefit from a widening basis (i.e. increasing prices for the outer contract and/or decreasing prices for the near contract).

Use of Bull Spread by Agricultural Processor

Assume an agricultural processor needs to secure raw materials at the lowest possible price to sell finished goods at the highest possible price. In this situation, the processor would structure a bull spread with two objectives:

- Lock in a favorable price for raw materials with the expectation that prices will increase (long).
- Lock in a favorable selling price for finished goods with the expectation that prices will decrease (short).

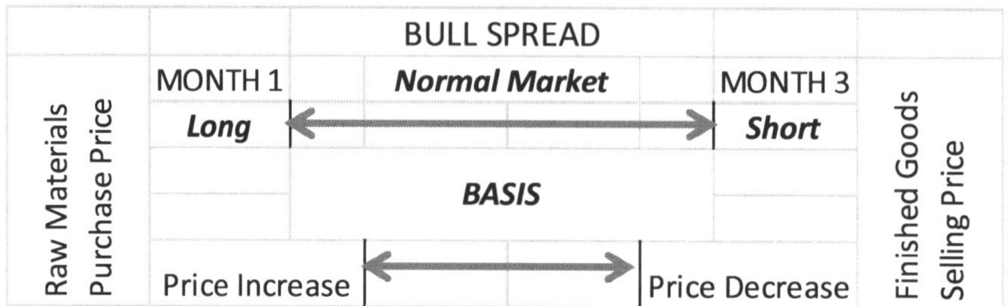

Types of Spread Orders

Intracommodity and Intercommodity

"Intra" refers to a spread in which both legs are for like commodities (such as Sept. soybeans and Dec. soybeans). This type of spread is also known as a calendar spread.

An "inter" spread is one in which one leg is for one commodity (such as a long in corn) and the other leg is for a different but related commodity (such as a short in live cattle).

Intradelivery and Interdelivery

The "delivery" portion of the spread order names refers to the month in which the contract matures or expires. "Intra" means each leg matures during the same delivery month, while "inter" means that the legs mature during two different delivery months. Note that an interdelivery spread is synonymous with an intracommodity or calendar spread.

Intramarket and Intermarket

The "market" portion of the spread order names refers to the exchange(s) on which an order is traded. "Intra" indicates that both legs trade on the same exchange, while "inter" indicates that each leg trades on a separate exchange. The Chicago Board of Trade (CBOT) and the Minneapolis Grain Exchange (MGEX) both offer an intermarket spread in wheat.

Speculators Provide Liquidity to Futures Market

Speculators provide liquidity to the futures market by accepting the risk of assuming the role of counterparty to hedgers. While many hedges are the result of two counterparties hedging opposite cash positions, many other positions involve only one hedge. Therefore, in order for the market to function efficiently and provide all traders with counterparties, speculators are a must. Without speculation, markets would be thinly traded, a condition that would result in exponentially more volatility and, in turn, more risk.

Profit/Loss Calculations for Speculative Trades

Example Calculations

Example 1

The yield on future month Eurodollar contracts is .325%. Assume that the yield declines to .310% in the contract delivery month. Calculate both the futures and the actual contract price, as well as the gross profit or loss of the position (assume $25 per basis point). Which position (long or short) benefits from the decline in yield?

The price is calculated as a 100-yield rate, so the contract price is 99.675 and the delivery month price is 99.690. The gain/(loss) is calculated as shown in the table below:

CME EURODOLLARS January 2013				
CONTRACT:	$	1,000,000		
MATURITY:	3	MONTHS		
QUOTE PRICE:	$25	PER BASIS POINT		
		ACTUAL RATES DECLINE		
		SHORT	LONG	
		MARCH	**JUNE**	
YIELD ON CONTRACT PRICE		0.325%	0.325%	
CONTRACT PRICE	sell	99.675	99.675	buy
ACTUAL YIELD IN DELIVERY MONTH		0.310%	0.310%	
CONTRACT PRICE IN DELIVERY MONTH	buy	99.690	99.690	sell
CHANGE		(0.0150)	0.0150	
GAIN/(LOSS)		$ (3,750)	$ 3,750	
Note: gain/(loss) = change / .0001 x $25				

Note that the long position benefits from rising prices that occur as a result of declining interest rates

Example 2

A trader enters into a Eurodollar bear spread contract in a normal market. The near-term contract yield is .350%, while the outer-term contract yield is .335%. Assume that the yield in the near-term delivery month rises to .360% and the outer-term rate remains essentially unchanged at .332%. Calculate the futures and actual contract prices and the gross profit on the net spread position.

The contract price is calculated as a 100-yield rate. The gross profit is calculated as shown in the table below. Note that a bear spread is structured to benefit from an expansion of the basis, which is also shown in the table below:

CME EURODOLLAR BEAR SPREAD						
CONTRACT:	$	1,000,000				
QUOTE PRICE:	$25	PER BASIS POINT				
		MONTH 1		MONTH 3		BASIS
YIELD ON CONTRACT PRICE		0.350%		0.335%		
CONTRACT PRICE	sell	99.650		99.665	buy	(0.015)
ACTUAL YIELD IN DELIVERY MONTH		0.360%		0.332%		
CONTRACT PRICE IN DELIVERY MONTH	buy	99.640		99.668	sell	(0.028)
CHANGE		0.0100		0.0030		
GROSS PROFIT/(LOSS)		$ 2,500	$	750		
Note: gain/(loss) = change / .0001 x $25						

Costs for Underlying Commodities

Trading in futures transactions does not exempt one from paying commissions and other fees. Aside from the costs of opening and closing a position, there are other types of costs for various underlying commodities (such as agricultural commodities and interest rates) that will affect gross profit. Costs for underlying agricultural commodities can include substantial delivery, inspection, and storage costs, among others. Costs for financial instruments include lesser costs, such as bank transfers and record keeping, as well as interest in situations where borrowed assets are used.

ROI

The return on investment (ROI), also known as return on equity or return on margin employed, is the ratio between the gross profit on a trade and the margin required to secure that trade:

- gross profit/(loss) = gain/(loss) on trade – commissions
- investment = margin per contract × number of contracts
- gross profit / investment = rate of return (on investment)

While it is conventional to treat commissions as a reduction in the gain or loss on a trade, the cost may alternately be considered an addition to the investment cost. In such cases, both the numerator and the denominator of the ROI calculation would be increased by the commission amount, resulting in a higher rate of return. Therefore, the more conservative approach is to treat commission as a cost that reduces gross profit.

Calculation of Gross Profit and Return on Equity

Example

Use the information below to calculate the gross profit and return on equity for a long position on a CME WTI Crude contract:

- margin: $5,100
- contract size: 1,000 barrels
- price: $93.56 (January)
- price: $94.72 (April)
- commission rate: 0.1%

CME QUOTE - WTI CRUDE OIL, FEB DELIVERY		
INITIAL MARGIN PER CONTRACT	$5,100	
PRICE:	$93.56	per barrel
CONTRACT SIZE	1,000	barrels
CONTRACT VALUE	$93,560	
COMMISSION RATE	0.10%	
JAN - Purchase 10 contracts April delivery	$93.56	$935,600
APR - Sell 10 contracts	$94.72	$947,200
GAIN/(LOSS)	$1.16	$11,600
Less: Commissions		$936
GROSS PROFIT		$10,664
INVESTMENT (MARGIN)		$51,000
RETURN ON INVESTMENT		**20.9%**
annualized		*83.6%*

Return on Investment (Equity/Margin) Calculation Examples

Grains (Soybeans)

COMMODITY: AGRICULTURAL (SOYBEANS)		PRICING UNIT:	CENTS PER BUSHEL	
CURRENT DATE: JAN 2013		INITIAL MARGIN:	$ 4,590	
FUTURES DATE: JUL 2013				
		SHORT HEDGE	**LONG HEDGE**	
FUTURES CONTRACT SIZE IN BUSHELS		5,000	5,000	
QUANTITY OF BUSHELS TO HEDGE		300,000	300,000	
NUMBER OF CONTRACTS REQUIRED		60	60	
CASH PRICE (January)		1,424	1,424	
FUTURES PRICE	*sell*	1,440	1,440	*buy*
CASH SETTLEMENT RESULT:				
ACTUAL CASH PRICE (July)		1,400	1,460	
FUTURES CONTRACT SETTLEMENT RESULT:				
FUTURES PRICE		1,440	1,440	
ACTUAL FUTURES CLOSE-OUT PRICE		1,400	1,460	
NET BENEFIT PER BUSHEL FROM HEDGE		40	20	
GROSS PROFIT		$ 120,000	$ 60,000	
INVESTMENT (MARGIN)		$ 275,400	$ 275,400	
RETURN ON INVESTMENT		**43.6%**	**21.8%**	
Note: commissions are ignored				
RECONCILIATION OF GROSS PROFIT:				
CONTRACT GAIN/(LOSS) PER BUSHEL		$ 0.4000	$ 0.2000	
MINIMUM PRICE TICK		$ 0.0025	$ 0.0025	
GAIN/(LOSS) DIVIDED BY MINIMUM PRICE TICK		160	80	
CONTRACT VALUE PER PRICE TICK		$ 12.50	$ 12.50	
GAIN/(LOSS) PER CONTRACT		$ 2,000	$ 1,000	
GROSS PROFIT		$ 120,000	$ 60,000	

Livestock (Live Cattle)

COMMODITY: LIVESTOCK (LIVE CATTLE)		PRICING UNIT:	CENTS PER POUND	
CURRENT DATE: FEB 2013		INITIAL MARGIN:	$ 1,350	
FUTURES DATE: AUG 2013				
		SHORT HEDGE	**LONG HEDGE**	
FUTURES CONTRACT SIZE IN POUNDS		40,000	40,000	
POUNDS TO HEDGE		600,000	600,000	
NUMBER OF CONTRACTS REQUIRED		15	15	
CASH PRICE (February)		124.950	124.950	
FUTURES PRICE	*sell*	129.525	129.525	*buy*
CASH SETTLEMENT RESULT:				
ACTUAL CASH PRICE IN AUGUST		127.250	131.450	
FUTURES CONTRACT SETTLEMENT RESULT:				
FUTURES PRICE		129.525	129.525	
ACTUAL FUTURES CLOSE-OUT PRICE		127.250	131.450	
NET BENEFIT PER POUND FROM HEDGE		2.275	1.925	
GROSS PROFIT		$ 13,650	$ 11,550	
INVESTMENT (MARGIN)		$ 20,250	$ 20,250	
RETURN ON INVESTMENT		**67.4%**	**57.0%**	
Note: commissions are ignored				
RECONCILIATION OF GROSS PROFIT:				
CONTRACT GAIN/(LOSS) PER POUND		$ 0.02275	$ 0.01925	
MINIMUM PRICE TICK		$ 0.00025	$ 0.00025	
GAIN/(LOSS) DIVIDED BY MINIMUM PRICE TICK		91	77	
CONTRACT VALUE PER PRICE TICK		$ 10.00	$ 10.00	
GAIN/(LOSS) PER CONTRACT		$ 910	$ 770	
GROSS PROFIT		$ 13,650	$ 11,550	

Foodstuffs (Cheese)

COMMODITY: FOODSTUFFS (CHEESE)		PRICING UNIT:	CENTS PER POUND	
CURRENT DATE: FEB 2013		INITIAL MARGIN:	$ 2,025	
FUTURES DATE: AUG 2013				
		SHORT HEDGE	**LONG HEDGE**	
FUTURES CONTRACT SIZE IN POUNDS		20,000	20,000	
POUNDS TO HEDGE		600,000	600,000	
NUMBER OF CONTRACTS REQUIRED		30	30	
CASH PRICE (February)		1.700	1.700	
FUTURES PRICE	*sell*	1.860	1.860	*buy*
CASH SETTLEMENT RESULT:				
ACTUAL CASH PRICE IN AUGUST		1.420	1.970	
FUTURES CONTRACT SETTLEMENT RESULT:				
FUTURES PRICE		1.860	1.860	
ACTUAL FUTURES CLOSE-OUT PRICE		1.420	1.970	
NET BENEFIT PER POUND FROM HEDGE		0.440	0.110	
NET BENEFIT IN USD		$ 2,640	$ 660	
INVESTMENT (MARGIN)		$ 60,750	$ 60,750	
RETURN ON INVESTMENT		**4.3%**	**1.1%**	
Note: commissions are ignored				
RECONCILIATION OF GROSS PROFIT:				
CONTRACT GAIN/(LOSS) PER POUND		$ 0.0044	$ 0.0011	
MINIMUM PRICE TICK		$ 0.0010	$ 0.0010	
GAIN/(LOSS) DIVIDED BY MINIMUM PRICE TICK		4.4	1.1	
CONTRACT VALUE PER PRICE TICK		$ 20.00	$ 20.00	
GAIN/(LOSS) PER CONTRACT		$ 88	$ 22	
GROSS PROFIT		$ 2,640	$ 660	

Metals (Silver)

COMMODITY: METALS (SILVER)		PRICING UNIT:	CENTS PER TROY OUNCE	
CURRENT DATE: JAN 2013		INITIAL MARGIN:	$ 12,100	
FUTURES DATE: JUL 2013				
		SHORT HEDGE	**LONG HEDGE**	
FUTURES CONTRACT SIZE IN TROY OUNCES		5,000	5,000	
OUNCES TO HEDGE		600,000	600,000	
NUMBER OF CONTRACTS REQUIRED		120	120	
CASH PRICE (January)		$ 32.147	$ 32.147	
FUTURES PRICE	*sell*	$ 32.287	$ 32.287	*buy*
CASH SETTLEMENT RESULT:				
ACTUAL CASH PRICE IN JULY		$ 27.442	$ 34.988	
FUTURES CONTRACT SETTLEMENT RESULT:				
FUTURES PRICE		$ 32.287	$ 32.287	
ACTUAL FUTURES CLOSE-OUT PRICE		$ 27.442	$ 34.988	
NET BENEFIT PER OUNCE FROM HEDGE		$ 4.845	$ 2.701	
NET BENEFIT IN USD		$ 29,070	$ 16,206	
INVESTMENT (MARGIN)		$ 1,452,000	$ 1,452,000	
RETURN ON INVESTMENT		**2.0%**	**1.1%**	
Note: commissions are ignored				
RECONCILIATION OF GROSS PROFIT:				
CONTRACT GAIN/(LOSS) PER TROY OUNCE		$ 0.0485	$ 0.0270	
MINIMUM PRICE TICK		$ 0.0050	$ 0.0050	
GAIN/(LOSS) DIVIDED BY MINIMUM PRICE TICK		9.69	5.402	
CONTRACT VALUE PER PRICE TICK		$ 25.00	$ 25.00	
GAIN/(LOSS) PER CONTRACT		$ 242	$ 135	
GROSS PROFIT		$ 29,070	$ 16,206	

Energy (Ethanol)

COMMODITY: ENERGY (ETHANOL)				
CURRENT DATE: FEB 2013		INITIAL MARGIN:	$ 4,455	
FUTURES DATE: AUG 2013				
PRICING UNIT: DOLLARS AND CENTS PER GALLON				
		SHORT HEDGE	**LONG HEDGE**	
FUTURES CONTRACT SIZE IN GALLONS		29,000	29,000	
GALLONS TO HEDGE		600,000	600,000	
NUMBER OF CONTRACTS REQUIRED		21	21	
CASH PRICE (February)		$ 2.375	$ 2.375	
FUTURES PRICE	*sell*	$ 2.198	$ 2.198	*buy*
CASH SETTLEMENT RESULT:				
ACTUAL CASH PRICE IN AUGUST		$ 2.146	$ 2.209	
FUTURES CONTRACT SETTLEMENT RESULT:				
FUTURES PRICE		$ 2.198	$ 2.198	
ACTUAL FUTURES CLOSE-OUT PRICE		$ 2.146	$ 2.209	
NET BENEFIT PER GALLON FROM HEDGE		$ 0.052	$ 0.011	
NET BENEFIT IN USD		$ 31,200	$ 6,600	
INVESTMENT (MARGIN)		$ 92,172	$ 92,172	
RETURN ON INVESTMENT		**33.8%**	**7.2%**	
Note: commissions are ignored				
RECONCILIATION OF GROSS PROFIT:				
CONTRACT GAIN/(LOSS) PER GALLON		$ 0.05200	$ 0.01100	
MINIMUM PRICE TICK		$ 0.00100	$ 0.00100	
GAIN/(LOSS) DIVIDED BY MINIMUM PRICE TICK		52	11	
CONTRACT VALUE PER PRICE TICK		$ 29.00	$ 29.00	
GAIN/(LOSS) PER CONTRACT		$ 1,508	$ 319	
GROSS PROFIT		$ 31,200	$ 6,600	

Lumber (Random Length)

COMMODITY: LUMBER (RANDOM LENGTH)				
CURRENT DATE: MAR 2013		INITIAL MARGIN:	$ 1,870	
FUTURES DATE: SEP 2013				
PRICING UNIT: DOLLARS PER THOUSAND BOARD FEET				
		SHORT HEDGE	**LONG HEDGE**	
FUTURES CONTRACT SIZE IN BOARD FEET		110,000	110,000	
BOARD FEET TO HEDGE		600,000	600,000	
NUMBER OF CONTRACTS REQUIRED		5	5	
CASH PRICE (March)		362.30	362.30	
FUTURES PRICE	*sell*	349.70	349.70	*buy*
CASH SETTLEMENT RESULT:				
ACTUAL CASH PRICE IN SEPTEMBER		342.60	358.10	
FUTURES CONTRACT SETTLEMENT RESULT:				
FUTURES PRICE		349.70	349.70	
ACTUAL FUTURES CLOSE-OUT PRICE		342.60	358.10	
NET BENEFIT PER THOUSAND BOARD FEET FROM HEDGE		7.10	8.40	
NET BENEFIT IN USD		$ 4,260	$ 5,040	
INVESTMENT (MARGIN)		$ 10,200	$ 10,200	
RETURN ON INVESTMENT		**41.8%**	**49.4%**	
Note: commissions are ignored				
RECONCILIATION OF GROSS PROFIT:				
CONTRACT GAIN/(LOSS) PER BUSHEL THOUSAND BOARD FEET		$ 7.10000	$ 8.40000	
MINIMUM PRICE TICK		$ 0.10000	$ 0.10000	
GAIN/(LOSS) DIVIDED BY MINIMUM PRICE TICK		71	84	
CONTRACT VALUE PER PRICE TICK		$ 11.00	$ 11.00	
GAIN/(LOSS) PER CONTRACT		$ 781	$ 924	
GROSS PROFIT		$ 4,260	$ 5,040	

T-Bonds (30 Year)

COMMODITY: U.S. TREASURY BONDS		INITIAL MARGIN:			$ 3,375	
CURRENT DATE: MAR 2013		ASSUMED COUPON RATE:			6.00%	
FUTURES DATE: SEP 2013		ASSUMED YEARS TO MATURITY:			15.0	
PRICING UNIT: PCTG OF PAR PLUS 32nds						
		SHORT HEDGE		**LONG HEDGE**		
		UNIT PRICE	**RATE OF INTEREST ***	**UNIT PRICE**	**RATE OF INTEREST ***	
FUTURES CONTRACT SIZE IN USD		$ 100,000		$ 100,000		
CASH PRICE (March)		146.27	*2.051%*	146.27	*2.051%*	
FUTURES PRICE	*sell*	144.11	*2.082%*	144.11	*2.082%*	*buy*
CASH SETTLEMENT RESULT:						
ACTUAL PRICE IN SEPTEMBER		143.08	*2.097%*	145.21	*2.066%*	
FUTURES CONTRACT SETTLEMENT RESULT:						
FUTURES PRICE		144.11		144.11		
ACTUAL FUTURES CLOSE-OUT PRICE		143.08		145.21		
NET BENEFIT FROM HEDGE		1.03	1 3/32	1.10	1 10/32	
		$ 1,093.75		$ 1,312.50		
INVESTMENT (MARGIN)		$ 3,375.00		$ 3,375.00		
RETURN ON INVESTMENT		**32.4%**		**38.9%**		
Note: commissions are ignored						
RECONCILIATION OF GROSS PROFIT:						
CONTRACT GAIN/(LOSS) POINTS		1.03		1.10		
MINIMUM PRICE TICK		1/32		1/32		
CONTRACT GAIN/(LOSS) IN 32NDS		35		33		
CONTRACT VALUE PER PRICE TICK		$ 31.250		$ 31.250		
GROSS PROFIT		$ 1,093.75		$ 1,031.25		

* *ESTIMATED: coupon rate divided by 2, divided by price, multiplied by 100*

T-Notes (5 Year)

COMMODITY: U.S. TREASURY NOTES (5 YEAR)			ASSUMED COUPON RATE		6.0%	
CURRENT DATE: MAR 2013			ASSUMED YEARS TO MAT		2.5	
FUTURES DATE: SEP 2013			INITIAL MARGIN:		$ 743	
PRICING UNIT: PCTG OF PAR PLUS 32nds & QTRS OF 32nds						
		SHORT HEDGE		**LONG HEDGE**		
		UNIT PRICE	**RATE OF INTEREST ***	**UNIT PRICE**	**RATE OF INTEREST ***	
FUTURES CONTRACT SIZE IN USD		$ 100,000		$ 100,000		
CASH PRICE (March)		124.072	*2.418%*	124.072	*2.418%*	
FUTURES PRICE	*sell*	123.054	*2.438%*	123.054	*2.438%*	*buy*
CASH SETTLEMENT RESULT:						
ACTUAL PRICE IN SEPTEMBER		122.042	*2.458%*	123.172	*2.436%*	
FUTURES CONTRACT SETTLEMENT RESULT:						
FUTURES PRICE		123.054		123.054		
ACTUAL FUTURES CLOSE-OUT PRICE		122.042		123.172		
NET BENEFIT FROM HEDGE		1.0120	2 1.25/32	0.1180	1 11.75/32	
		$ 523.44		$ 195.31		
INVESTMENT (MARGIN)		$ 743.00		$ 743.00		
RETURN ON INVESTMENT		**70.4%**		**26.3%**		
Note: commissions are ignored						
RECONCILIATION OF GROSS PROFIT:						
CONTRACT GAIN/(LOSS) POINTS		1.012		0.118		
MINIMUM PRICE TICK		1/(32X4)		1/(32X4)		
CONTRACT GAIN/(LOSS) IN 128THS		67		25		
CONTRACT VALUE PER PRICE TICK		$ 7.8125		$ 7.8125		
GROSS PROFIT		$ 523.44		$ 195.31		

* *ESTIMATED: coupon rate divided by 2, divided by price, multiplied by 100*

T-Bills (13 Week)

COMMODITY: U.S. TREASURY BILLS (13 WEEK)		INITIAL MARGIN:		$ 405		
CURRENT DATE: MAR 2013						
FUTURES DATE: SEP 2013						
PRICING UNIT: 100 MINUS ANNUALIZED DISCOUNT RATE						
		SHORT HEDGE		**LONG HEDGE**		
		UNIT PRICE	**INTEREST ***	**UNIT PRICE**	**RATE OF INTEREST ***	
FUTURES CONTRACT SIZE IN USD		$ 1,000,000		$ 1,000,000		
CASH PRICE (Based on March)		99.270	*0.730%*	99.270	*0.730%*	
FUTURES PRICE	*sell*	99.255	*0.745%*	99.255	*0.745%*	*buy*
CASH SETTLEMENT RESULT:						
ACTUAL PRICE IN SEPTEMBER		99.245	*0.755%* increase	99.285	*0.715%* decrease	
FUTURES CONTRACT SETTLEMENT RESULT:						
FUTURES PRICE		99.255		99.255		
ACTUAL FUTURES CLOSE-OUT PRICE		99.245		99.285		
NET BENEFIT FROM HEDGE		0.010		0.030		
		$ 25.00		$ 75.00		
INVESTMENT (MARGIN)		$ 405.00		$ 405.00		
RETURN ON INVESTMENT		**6.2%**		**18.5%**		
Note: commissions are ignored						
RECONCILIATION OF GROSS PROFIT:						
CONTRACT GAIN/(LOSS) POINTS		0.010		0.030		
MINIMUM PRICE TICK		0.005		0.005		
CONTRACT GAIN/(LOSS) IN 32NDS		2		6		
CONTRACT VALUE PER PRICE TICK		$ 12.500		$ 12.500		
GROSS PROFIT		$ 25.00		$ 75.00		

* *ESTIMATED: coupon rate divided by 2, divided by price, multiplied by 100*

Municipals

COMMODITY: MUNICIPALS (BOND BUYER INDEX)				PRICING UNIT: PCTG OF PAR PLUS 32nds		
CURRENT DATE: MAR 2010				ASSUMED COUPON RATE:	4.0%	
FUTURES DATE: SEP 2010				INITIAL MARGIN:	$ 4,450	
		SHORT HEDGE		LONG HEDGE		
		UNIT PRICE	RATE OF INTEREST *	UNIT PRICE	RATE OF INTEREST *	
FUTURES CONTRACT SIZE IN USD		$ 100,000		$ 100,000		
CASH PRICE (Based on March)		115.25	*1.735%*	115.25	*1.735%*	
FUTURES PRICE	*sell*	117.10	*1.708%*	117.10	*1.708%*	*buy*
CASH SETTLEMENT RESULT:						
ACTUAL PRICE IN SEPTEMBER		116.04	*1.724%*	118.28	*1.691%*	
FUTURES CONTRACT SETTLEMENT RESULT:						
FUTURES PRICE		117.10		117.10		
ACTUAL FUTURES CLOSE-OUT		116.04		118.28		
NET BENEFIT FROM HEDGE		1.06	1 6/32	1.18	1 18/32	
		$ 1,187.50		$ 1,562.50		
INVESTMENT (MARGIN)		$ 4,450.00		$ 4,450.00		
RETURN ON INVESTMENT		**26.7%**		**35.1%**		
Note: commissions are ignored						
RECONCILIATION OF GROSS PROFIT:						
CONTRACT GAIN/(LOSS) POINTS		1.06		1.18		
MINIMUM PRICE TICK		1/32		1/32		
CONTRACT GAIN/(LOSS) IN 32NDS		38		50		
CONTRACT VALUE PER PRICE TICK		$ 31.25		$ 31.25		
GROSS PROFIT		$ 1,187.50		$ 1,562.50		

* *ESTIMATED: coupon rate divided by 2, divided by price, multiplied by 100*

Eurodollars

COMMODITY: EURODOLLARS			INITIAL MARGIN:		$ 338		
CURRENT DATE: MAR 2013							
FUTURES DATE: SEP 2013							
PRICING UNIT: 100 MINUS ANNUALIZED DISCOUNT RATE							
		SHORT HEDGE		**LONG HEDGE**			
		UNIT PRICE	**RATE OF INTEREST ***	**UNIT PRICE**	**RATE OF INTEREST ***		
FUTURES CONTRACT SIZE IN USD		$ 1,000,000		$ 1,000,000			
CASH PRICE (Based on March)		99.695	*0.305%*	99.695	*0.305%*		
FUTURES PRICE	*sell*	99.690	*0.310%*	99.690	*0.310%*	*buy*	
CASH SETTLEMENT RESULT:							
ACTUAL PRICE IN SEPTEMBER		99.660	*0.340%*	99.699	*0.301%*		
			increase		decrease		
FUTURES CONTRACT SETTLEMENT RESULT:							
FUTURES PRICE		99.690		99.690			
ACTUAL FUTURES CLOSE-OUT PRICE		99.660		99.699			
NET BENEFIT FROM HEDGE		0.030		0.009			
		$ 75.00		$ 22.50			
INVESTMENT (MARGIN)		$ 338.00		$ 338.00			
RETURN ON INVESTMENT		**22.2%**		**6.7%**			
Note: commissions are ignored							
RECONCILIATION OF GROSS PROFIT:							
CONTRACT GAIN/(LOSS) POINTS		0.0300		0.0090			
MINIMUM PRICE TICK		0.0025		0.0025			
CONTRACT GAIN/(LOSS) IN 32NDS		12		4			
CONTRACT VALUE PER PRICE TICK		$ 6.250		$ 6.250			
GROSS PROFIT		$ 75.00		$ 22.50			

* *ESTIMATED: coupon rate divided by 2, divided by price, multiplied by 100*

Currencies (USD/JPY)

COMMODITY: CURRENCY RATES JPY:USD		PRICING UNIT: .10 INDEX POINTS X $25				
CURRENT DATE: MAR 2013		CONTRACT VALUE: INDEX PRICE X $250				
FUTURES DATE: SEP 2013		INITIAL MARGIN:		$ 2,475		
		SHORT HEDGE		**LONG HEDGE**		
		UNIT PRICE	**1 USD**	**UNIT PRICE**	**1 USD**	
FUTURES CONTRACT SIZE IN JPY		¥12,500,000		¥12,500,000		
CASH PRICE (Based on available Mar. forward contract)		$ 0.0112740	88.70	$ 0.0112740	88.70	
AVAILABLE HEDGE: FUTURES CONTRACT AT A PRICE OF.....	*sell*	$ 0.0112830	88.63	$ 0.0112830	88.63	*buy*
CASH SETTLEMENT RESULT:						
ACTUAL PRICE IN SEPTEMBER		$ 0.0111920	89.35	$ 0.0114210	87.56	
FUTURES CONTRACT SETTLEMENT RESULT:						
FUTURES CONTRACT PRICE		$ 0.0112830	88.63	$0.01128300	88.63	
ACTUAL FUTURES CLOSE-OUT PRICE (IN DELIVERY MONTH)		$ 0.0111920	89.35	$0.01142100	87.56	
NET BENEFIT FROM HEDGE		$ 0.0000910		$ 0.0001380		
		$ 1,137.50		$ 1,725.00		
INVESTMENT (MARGIN)		$ 2,475		2,475.00		
RETURN ON INVESTMENT		**46.0%**		**69.7%**		
Note: commissions are ignored						
RECONCILIATION OF GROSS PROFIT:						
CONTRACT GAIN/(LOSS) POINTS		$ 0.000091		$ 0.000138		
MINIMUM PRICE TICK		$ 0.000001		$ 0.000001		
GAIN/(LOSS) DIVIDED BY MINIMUM PRICE TICK		91		138		
CONTRACT VALUE PER PRICE TICK		$ 12.50		$ 12.50		
GROSS PROFIT		$ 1,137.50		$ 1,725.00		

Stock Indices (S&P 500)

COMMODITY: STOCK INDEX S&P 500		PRICING UNIT: .10 INDEX POINTS X $25		
CURRENT DATE: MAR 2013		CONTRACT VALUE: INDEX PRICE X $250		
FUTURES DATE: SEP 2013		INITIAL MARGIN:	$ 17,500	
		SHORT HEDGE	**LONG HEDGE**	
		UNIT PRICE	**UNIT PRICE**	
FUTURES CONTRACT SIZE IN USD		$ 372,350	$ 372,350	
CASH PRICE (Based on March)		1,489.40	1,489.40	
FUTURES PRICE	*sell*	1,475.80	1,475.80	*buy*
CASH SETTLEMENT RESULT:				
ACTUAL PRICE IN SEPTEMBER		1,442.50	1,502.25	
FUTURES CONTRACT SETTLEMENT RESULT:				
FUTURES PRICE		1,475.80	1,475.80	
ACTUAL FUTURES CLOSE-OUT PRICE		1,442.50	1,502.25	
NET BENEFIT FROM HEDGE		33.30	26.45	
		$ 8,325.00	$ 6,612.50	
INVESTMENT (MARGIN)		$ 17,500	$ 17,500	
RETURN ON INVESTMENT		**47.6%**	**37.8%**	
Note: commissions are ignored				
RECONCILIATION OF GROSS PROFIT:				
CONTRACT GAIN/(LOSS) POINTS		33.30	26.45	
MINIMUM PRICE TICK		$ 0.10	$ 0.10	
GAIN/(LOSS) DIVIDED BY MINIMUM PRICE TICK		333	264.5	
CONTRACT VALUE PER PRICE TICK		$ 25.00	$ 25.00	
GROSS PROFIT		$ 8,325.00	$ 6,612.50	

Comparing Taxable and Tax-Free Intercommodity Trades

When calculating a comparative ROE for two intercommodity trades (one that is taxable and one that is tax free), the tax effect must be considered. There are two options for comparing a taxable and a tax-free transaction. The taxable amount must be reduced to adjust for the tax effect, or the tax-free amount must be similarly increased.

- calculation for a taxable transaction: taxable amount × (1 – tax rate) = tax-free amount
- calculation for a tax-free transaction: tax-free amount / (1 – tax rate) = taxable amount

Either calculation (but not both) will allow for an accurate comparison between commodities.

Trading Applications

Appropriate Speculative Futures Trade Recommendations

In a trading environment where prices are expected to increase, a long position is recommended (buy). If prices are expected to decrease, a short position is recommended (sell).

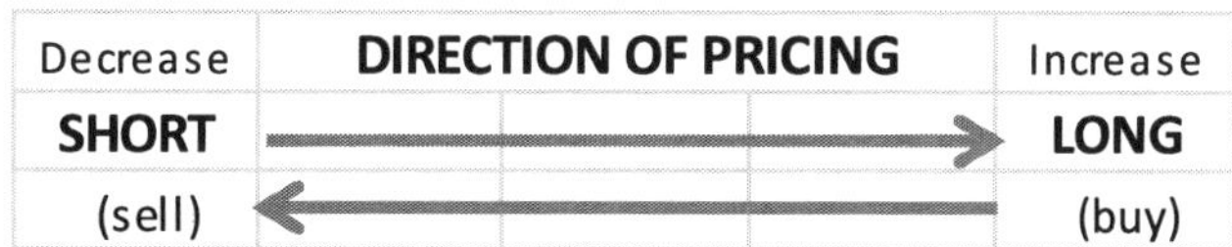

Recommendations for Changes in Basis

A spread position is recommended if a trader is speculating on changes in the basis. Two types of spreads are available to take advantage of a narrowing (bull spread) or widening (bear spread) of the basis:

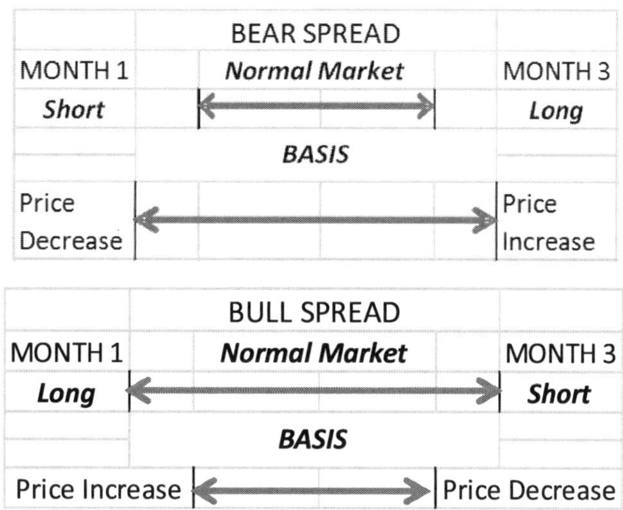

Stop Order

A stop order is an instruction to execute a trade when a price trigger is reached. In effect, when the trigger price is reached, the stop order is converted to a market order. The intent of the trader is to confirm the direction of the market prior to actually executing the order. For example, a buy stop (or buying on the stop) executes a buy order after the market has moved upward in price. A sell stop executes a sell after the market has moved downward in price.

Stop Limit Order

The keyword in the term stop limit order is "limit." The trade will only execute at the limit order or better (it does not convert to a market order). In contrast, a stop order will execute at the next available market price once the trigger price is reached. In this instance, a trader has established a specific target price rather than a general market direction.

OCO

A one cancels the other (OCO) order has two order legs. As the name implies, one leg is cancelled when the other leg is executed.

For example, assume crude oil is selling at $90 per barrel and an OCO order is entered as follows:

- sell $88.50 stop;
- sell $92.00 limit

The sell stop would be executed if the price falls to $88.50 (avoiding further losses), and the limit order would be cancelled. However, if the price does not fall and instead rises to $92, the trade would be executed (locking in gains). If neither occurs, the trade would expire when the market closes.

Pyramiding

Pyramiding is a trading strategy whereby profits earned on existing positions are automatically used to increase position size. The number of contracts added to increase position size typically grows progressively smaller. For example, in a rising market, a trader may use profits to add X number of contracts, then $X - 1$, then $X - 2$, etc. (assuming the price trend continues).

Option Hedging, Speculating, Spreading

Option Theory

Options Contract vs. Futures Contract

A trader who purchases an options contract has the right but not the obligation to purchase or sell a security prior to an expiration date. A futures contract is an obligation to take some action related to the underlying commodity. The trader must deliver the commodity, accept delivery, settle for cash, or liquidate (offset). In contrast, the holder of an options contract has a right to take some action related to the underlying commodity, but is not obligated to do so. In practice, in the money contracts will be executed, while out of the money contracts are worthless, and will therefore be allowed to expire.

Sectors That Have Commodities for Which Options Contracts Are Available

Options contracts are available for many (but not all) of the major commodities within the following sectors:

- agricultural (corn, soybeans, wheat, live cattle, lean hogs)
- energy (crude oil, natural gas, heating oil, gasoline)
- equity index (S&P 500, NASDAQ, DJIA)
- foreign exchange (JPY, EUR, GBP, AUD, CAD, CHF:USD)
- interest rates (Eurodollar, T-note, T-bond)
- metals (gold, silver, copper, platinum, palladium)

Party to Option Contract with the Greatest Risk of Loss

The seller or writer of an option bears the full obligation to meet the rights of the buyer (upon exercise), and thus has the greatest risk of loss. A seller or writer who engages in an option without an underlying position in the cash market is said to be "naked." A subsequent exercise by the holder creates even greater risk for the seller, as the underlying commodity must be acquired in order to fulfill the contract.

Puts and Calls from Perspectives of Buyers and Sellers/Writers

A buyer of a call has the right to buy the underlying commodity, and seeks to benefit from rising prices. A buyer of a put has the right to sell the underlying commodity, and seeks to benefit from declining prices. A seller of a call has the obligation to sell the underlying commodity if the call is exercised, and seeks to benefit from premium income. A seller of a put has the obligation to buy the underlying commodity if the put is exercised, and also seeks to benefit from premium income.

OPTION	OWNER (Purchaser)	PRICES RISE	PRICES FALL	SELLER (Writer)
PUT	Sell to writer at strike price X within period Y	*No exercise as can sell at market price which is higher than strike price*	*Put gains in value; can exercise as strike price is higher than market price*	Buy from owner at strike price X within period Y
CALL	Buy from writer at strike price X within period Y	*Call gains in value; can exercise as strike price is higher than market price*	*No exercise as can sell at market price which is higher than strike price*	Sell to owner at strike price X within period Y

Long and Short Positions

CHARACTERISTIC	LONG (BUYER)	SHORT (SELLER/WRITER)
RISK	*LIMITED*	*INCREASED*
LEVERAGE	*INCREASED*	*LIMITED*
LOSS	*LIMITED*	*INCREASED*

A buyer or holder of an option has the right to exercise it, but will do so only if it is profitable (in the money). If the option remains out of the money, the buyer/holder will allow it to expire, as it is worthless. Risk is minimal. The opportunity for leverage increases as the price of the underlying commodity undergoes favorable changes. Loss is limited to the premium paid to buy the position. The seller bears the risk of exercise, and is obligated to deliver. Leverage is somewhat nonexistent, as the profit is limited to the premium received from the buyer; the risk of loss can be substantial if changes in pricing are unfavorable.

Put and Call Actions

A call is an option to buy, and it would be exercised at any price above the strike price. A put is an option to sell, and it would be exercised at any price below the strike price.

OPTION OWNED BY INVESTOR	ACTION IF PRICE OF UNDERLYING ASSET ON EXPIRATION DATE IS,		
	GREATER THAN OPTION PRICE	EQUAL TO THE OPTION PRICE	BELOW THE OPTION PRICE
CALL	*EXERCISE*	*NO ACTION OR ALLOW TO EXPIRE*	*ALLOW TO EXPIRE*
PUT	*ALLOW TO EXPIRE*	*NO ACTION OR ALLOW TO EXPIRE*	*EXERCISE*

Option Price

The intrinsic value of an option is the difference between the market price of the underlying commodity and the strike price if the option is exercised (the amount by which the option is in the money). Another factor influencing the price of an option is the time value, which is essentially the probability that an option will reach in the money status. For example, two options with the same strike price would be expected to be priced differently depending upon the length of time to expiration. As an option approaches its expiration date, the time value diminishes and approaches zero.

Single Security

The Commodity Futures Modernization Act (CFMA) includes authorization for single security (or stock) futures as a new kind of equity/futures hybrid security. Single security (or stock) futures in the U.S. authorized by the CFMA represent contracts for lots of multiple shares of a single security (i.e. 100 shares), such as common stock, American depository receipts (ADRs), exchange traded funds (ETFs), and closed end mutual funds (CEMFs). Contracts must be settled through delivery; the seller must make and the buyer must accept delivery. Margin requirements are regulated by statutes rather than by individual exchanges. Trading activity is subject to the regulations of both the Securities Exchange Commission (SEC) and the Commodity Futures Trading Commission (CFTC). Enforcement is delegated to the Financial Industry Regulatory Authority (FINRA) and the National Futures Association (NFA).

Options Offset Prior to Settlement

Options can be offset prior to settlement (assuming the appropriate terms are available in the market), but only through the purchase or sale of the same type of option. That is, a long put can only be offset with a short put; a long call can only be offset with a short call.

Option Hedge Strategies/Calculations

Payoff Scenarios

Long and Short Futures Contracts

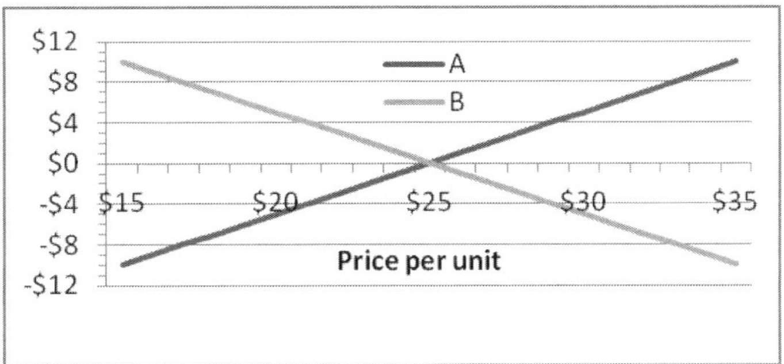

The graph is a representation of the payoff scenarios for a long futures contract and a short futures contract. The data indicate a purchase price of $25 (gain/loss is zero). Line A represents the long contract, which gains value as the price increases and loses value as the price decreases. Conversely, line B represents the short contract, which loses value as the price increases and gains value as the price decreases.

Long and Short Call Options

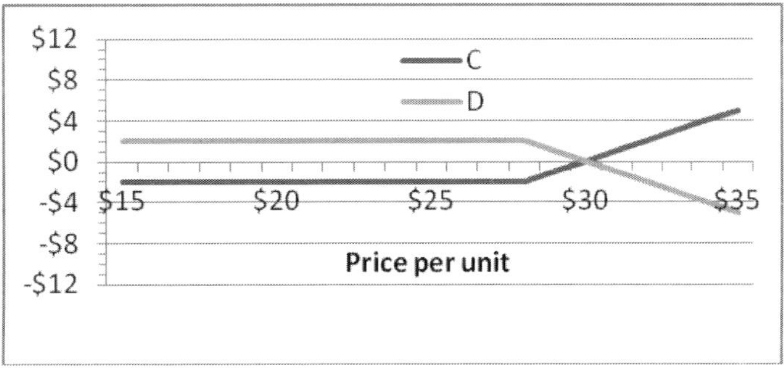

The graph is a representation of the payoff scenarios for a long and a short call option. The data indicate a strike price of $28 and a premium of $2. Line C represents the long call option. The premium paid for this option is $2, and the at the money price is $30 (strike plus premium). The option continues to gain value (in the money) as the price increases. Line D represents the short call option. The premium received for this option is $2, and the price at which the call is at the money for the holder is also $30. At this point, the writer of the option enters a negative position due to the possibility of exercise. The option continues to lose value as the price decreases.

Long and Short Put Options

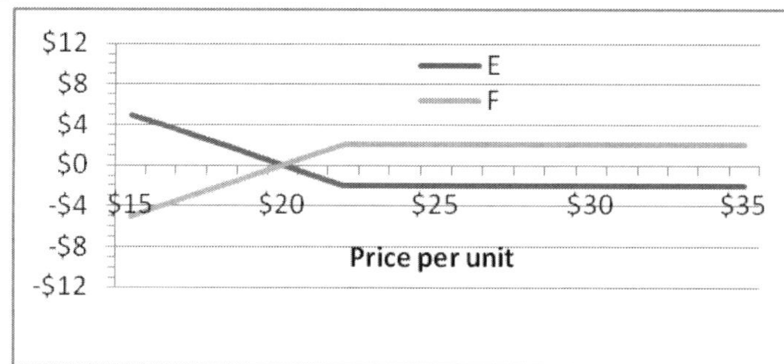

The graph is a representation of the payoff scenarios for a long and a short put option. The data indicate a strike price of $22 and a premium amount of $2. Line E represents the long put option. The premium paid is $2, and the at the money price is $20 (strike minus premium). The option continues to gain value (in the money) as the price declines. Line F represents the short put option. The premium received is $2, and the price at which the option is at the money for the holder is $20. At this point, the writer of the option enters a negative position due to the possibility of exercise. The option continues to lose value as the price declines.

Long Put vs. Short Futures

A long put will continue to gain value as the market price falls beyond the strike price. There is no downside risk other than the cost of the premium. A short future will gain value immediately as the price falls, but is also exposed to continuing losses at any point above the market price at inception.

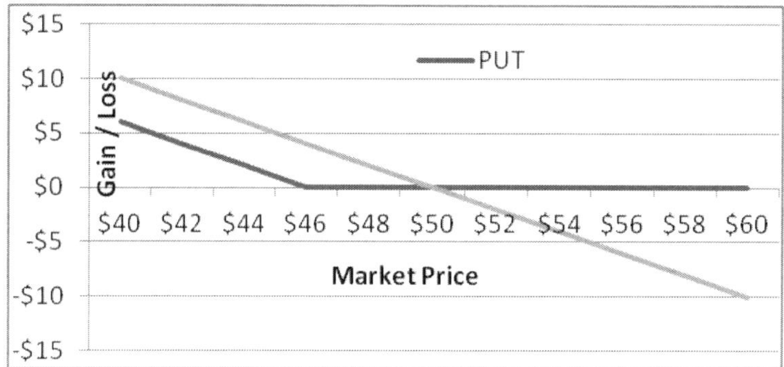

Long Call vs. Long Futures

A long call will continue to gain value as the market price rises beyond the strike price. There is no downside risk other than the cost of the premium. A long future will gain value immediately as the price rises, but is also exposed to continuing losses at any point below the market price at inception. The following example assumes a current market price of $50 and a call strike price of $54:

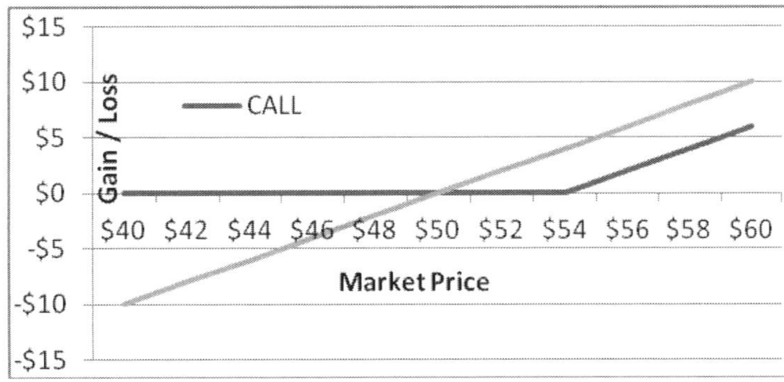

Options and Futures Once Breakeven Point Is Reached

The futures position offers unlimited (within the expiry period) upside potential at all prices either above (long) or below (short) the market price at inception. Options also offer unlimited (within the expiry period) upside potential, but only after the strike price is exceeded. The key difference between the two strategies is related to risk. Options can expire worthless if prices move adversely, while futures will experience losses.

Option Speculative Strategies/Calculations

Long Call and Long Futures

As hedges, both a long call and a long futures seek to protect the underlying short position, meaning there is a need to acquire the underlying commodity at the best price. A call will gain value at any price above the strike price; downside loss is limited to the premium paid. A futures will gain value at any price above market at inception; downside loss is incurred at any price below inception, and also includes commissions and margin.

LONG CALL VS. LONG FUTURES		
PRICES INCREASE	***PRICES DECREASE***	
Short position will lose; call value will increase (Intrinsic + Time Value) and can be exercised	Short position will gain; call will not be exercised	***PURCHASE A CALL***
PREMIUM PAID ON CALL (COST)		
Short position will lose; futures increase unlimited	Short position will gain; futures subject to margin call	***PURCHASE FUTURES***

The table below shows the profitability, ROI, and breakeven point for a long call and a long futures in various pricing scenarios. Note that there are continuing losses for futures as prices fall, while the maximum loss for a call is limited to the premium.

LONG CALL VS. LONG FUTURES							
		strike	*market*	*prem/margin*			
OPTIONS:	100	$26	$28	$4			
FUTURES:	100	NA	$26	$500	(1 contract)		

POSITION		**MARKET PRICING**					
		$24	**$26**	**$28**	**$30**	**$32**	**$34**
CALLS	Profit	-$400	-$400	-$200	$0	$200	$400
	ROI	-100%	-100%	-50%	0%	50%	100%
		Breakeven price:		**$30.00**			
FUTURES	Profit	-$200	$0	$200	$400	$600	$800
	ROI	-40%	0%	40%	80%	120%	160%
		Breakeven price:		**NA**			

note: commissions ignored

Long Put and Short Futures

As hedges, both a long put and a short futures seek to protect an underlying long position from a decline in prices. A long put will gain value at any price below the strike price; the downside risk is limited to the premium paid. A short futures will gain value at any price below the market price at inception; downside loss is incurred at any price above the market, and also includes commissions and margin.

LONG PUT VS. SHORT FUTURES		
	PRICES DECREASE	***PRICES INCREASE***
PURCHASE A PUT	Long position will lose; value of put will increase and can be exercised	Long position will gain; put will not be exercised
	PREMIUM PAID ON PUT (COST)	
SELL FUTURES	Long position will lose; futures increase unlimited	Long position will gain; futures subject to margin call

The table below shows the profitability, ROI, and breakeven point for a long put and a short futures in various pricing scenarios. Note that there are continuing losses for futures as prices increase, while the maximum loss for a put is limited to the premium.

LONG PUT VS. SHORT FUTURES							
		strike	*market*	*prem/margin*			
OPTIONS:	100	$26	$28	$4			
FUTURES:	100	NA	$26	$500	(1 contract)		
POSITION		**MARKET PRICING**					
		$22	**$24**	**$26**	**$28**	**$30**	**$32**
PUTS	Profit	$0	-$200	-$400	-$400	-$400	-$400
	ROI	0%	-50%	-100%	-100%	-100%	-100%
		Breakeven price:		**$22.00**			
FUTURES	Profit	$400	$200	$0	-$200	-$400	-$600
	ROI	80%	40%	0%	-40%	-80%	-120%
		Breakeven price:		**NA**			
note: commissions ignored							

Synthetic Long Put

A synthetic long put is a combination of a long call and a short futures, and provides the same result as an outright long put. The position is designed to profit from price decreases. However, the long call serves to offset losses on the futures if prices increase. The important caveat is that the strike price for all positions must be the same.

LONG CALL & SHORT FUTURES (SYNTHETIC LONG PUT)		
PRICES INCREASE	***PRICES DECREASE***	
Short position will lose; call value will increase (Intrinsic + Time Value) and can be exercised	Short position will gain; call will not be exercised	***PURCHASE A CALL***
PREMIUM PAID ON CALL (COST)		
Long position will gain; futures subject to margin call	Long position will lose; futures increase unlimited	***SELL FUTURES***

The table below shows the profitability, ROI, and breakeven point for a synthetic long put in various pricing scenarios. Note that the combined profitability for both positions is the same as what would be calculated for a separate long put.

LONG CALL & SHORT FUTURES (Synthetic Long Put)							
		strike	*market*	*rem/margin*			
OPTIONS	100	$26	$28	$4			
FUTURES:	100	NA	$26	$500	(1 contract)		
POSITION		**MARKET PRICING**					
		$22	**$24**	**$26**	**$28**	**$30**	**$32**
CALLS	Profit	-$400	-$400	-$400	-$200	$0	$200
	ROI	-100%	-100%	-100%	-50%	0%	50%
		Breakeven price		**$30.00**			
FUTURES	Profit	$400	$200	$0	-$200	-$400	-$600
	ROI	80%	40%	0%	-40%	-80%	-120%
		Breakeven price		NA			
= LONG PUT		***$0***	***-$200***	***-$400***	***-$400***	***-$400***	***-$400***
note: commissions ignored							

Long Call

The long call feature of a synthetic long put is designed to offset losses from the short futures in the event of price increases:

	strike:	*$26*		*market*			
	$22	**$24**	**$26**	**$27**	**$28**	**$30**	**$32**
LONG CALL	$0	$0	$0	$1	$2	$4	$6
SHORT FUTURES	$4	$2	$0	-$1	-$2	-$4	-$6

Synthetic Long Call

A synthetic long call is a combination of a long put and a long futures, and provides the same result as an outright long call. The position is intended to profit from price increases. However, the long put serves to offset futures losses in the event of price decreases. The maximum loss is limited to the premium paid. The important caveat is that the strike price for all positions must be the same.

LONG PUT & LONG FUTURES (SYNTHETIC LONG CALL)		
	PRICES DECREASE	*PRICES INCREASE*
PURCHASE A PUT	Long position will lose; value of put will increase and can be exercised	Long position will gain; put will not be exercised
	PREMIUM PAID ON PUT (COST)	
PURCHASE FUTURES	Short position will gain; futures subject to margin call	Short position will lose; futures increase unlimited

The table below shows the profitability, ROI, and breakeven point for a synthetic long call in various pricing scenarios.

LONG PUT & LONG FUTURES (Synthetic Long Call)							
		strike	*market*	*rem/margin*			
OPTIONS	100	$26	$28	$4			
FUTURES:	100	NA	$26	$500	(1 contract)		
POSITION		**MARKET PRICING**					
		$24	**$26**	**$28**	**$30**	**$32**	**$34**
PUTS	Profit	-$200	-$400	-$400	-$400	-$400	-$400
	ROI	-50%	-100%	-100%	-100%	-100%	-100%
		Breakeven price		**$22.00**			
FUTURES	Profit	-$200	$0	$200	$400	$600	$800
	ROI	-40%	0%	40%	80%	120%	160%
		Breakeven price		**NA**			
= LONG CALL		***-$400***	***-$400***	***-$200***	***$0***	***$200***	***$400***
note: commissions ignored							

Long Put

The long put feature of a synthetic long call is designed to offset losses from the long futures in the event of price decreases.

	strike:	*$26*		*market*			
	$20	**$22**	**$24**	**$27**	**$28**	**$30**	**$32**
LONG PUT	$6	$4	$2	$0	$0	$0	$0
LONG FUTURES	-$6	-$4	-$2	$1	$2	$4	$6

Synthetic Short Put

A synthetic short put is a combination of a short covered call and a long futures, and will provide the same result as an outright short put. The position is intended to protect an underlying long (covered) position from price decreases, and to profit from premium income. The long futures position protects the premium income in the event of price increases. In the event that the call is exercised, the trader is covered via the long position.

LONG FUTURES & SHORT COVERED CALL (SYNTHETIC SHORT PUT)		
	PRICES DECREASE	*PRICES INCREASE*
PURCHASE FUTURES	Short position will gain; futures subject to margin call	Short position will lose; futures increase unlimited
SELL A COVERED CALL	Long position will lose; call will not be exercised	Long (covered) position will gain but exercise will require delivery though not at higher cost
	PREMIUM RECEIVED FROM CALL (INCOME)	

The table below shows the profitability, ROI, and breakeven point for a synthetic short put in various pricing scenarios.

LONG FUTURES & SHORT COVERED CALL (Synthetic Short Put)								
		strike	*market*	*rem/margin*				
OPTIONS	100	$26	$28	$4				
FUTURES:	100	NA	$26	$500	(1 contract)			
POSITION		**MARKET PRICING**						
		$22	**$24**	**$26**	**$28**	**$30**	**$32**	**$34**
CALL	Profit	$400	$400	$400	$200	$0	-$200	-$400
	ROI	100%	100%	100%	50%	0%	-50%	-100%
		Breakeven price		**$30.00**				
FUTURES	Profit	-$400	-$200	$0	$200	$400	$600	$800
	ROI	-80%	-40%	0%	40%	80%	120%	160%
		Breakeven price		**NA**				
= SHORT PUT		***$0***	***$200***	***$400***	***$400***	***$400***	***$400***	***$400***
note: commissions ignored								

Synthetic Option

A synthetic option is created by combining a futures position and an outright option position in a single order. The combined effect of each of the two legs provides a result that is equivalent to a single outright option.

A long call and a short put will be profitable in a period of rising prices. The equivalent synthetic of each is as follows:

- Long Call = Long Futures + Long Put
- Short Put = Long Futures + Short Call

A long put and a short call will be profitable in a period of declining prices. The equivalent synthetic of each is as follows:

- Long Put = Short Futures + Long Call
- Short Call = Short Futures + Short Put

Conversion

Conversion is the term used when a trader, recognizing pricing inconsistencies between the two components of a synthetic position and the related outright position, combines short and long positions to profit from the arbitrage. For example, in a situation where the price of a long call is unfavorable compared to that of the synthetic components of a long futures and a long put, the trader would sell the call and buy the futures and the put. This also has the effect of forcing prices back to parity.

Reverse Conversion

Reverse conversion and conversion are opposite positions, but the desired result is the same. For example, in a situation where the long put is priced unfavorably compared to the synthetic components of a short futures and a long call, the trader would sell the put, buy the call, and sell the futures. As with the conversion process, reverse conversion has the effect of forcing prices back to parity.

Put/Call Parity in Options Pricing

Put/call parity is related to the practice of conversion/reverse conversion, which allows traders to take advantage of pricing inconsistencies between synthetic options and the related outright contract. The principle of put/call parity is that the price of the two combined contracts of a synthetic must be equal to the price of the outright contract. For example, a synthetic long call is a combination of a long futures and a long put. Parity means that the combined price of the long futures and the long put is always the same as that of the outright long call. Whenever inconsistencies arise, the process of conversion or reverse conversion will force the price back to parity.

Roll Forward

Roll forward is a trading strategy in which expiring contracts are liquidated and a new contract is immediately purchased. In effect, each expiring contract is rolled forward.

Option Spread Strategies/Calculations

Call Option Spreads

An option spread is a position involving the purchase of one option and the sale of another. The three types of call option spreads are:

- Price spread – A call is purchased at one price, while a different call is sold at a different price.
- Calendar – A call that expires on a certain date is purchased, while another call that expires on a different date is sold.
- Diagonal – This is a combination of a price spread and a calendar spread. Both the short and long positions have different prices and expiry dates.

Option Put Spread and Option Call Spread

Both puts and calls can be used to develop a spread to protect underlying positions and thereby minimize risk. Like calls, puts can be used to structure spreads (a combination of short and long positions) based on price, expiry dates, or a combination thereof.

Vertical Credit Spread and Vertical Debit Spread

A vertical credit spread and a vertical debit spread are said to be mirror images of each other. Both credit and debit spreads are considered vertical because they use the same option type (call or put) in two different positions (long or short). Both are designed such that the maximum profit and loss are limited by the price range of the two option types (puts or calls). A credit spread (bull put or bear call) limits profitability to the net premium income, and it limits losses to the adverse change in price. A debit spread is a mirror image of the credit spread because it limits losses to the net premium expense, and it also limits profitability to the beneficial change in price.

Bull Put

A bull put is a vertical credit spread, and the trader seeks to profit from a widening of the basis. That is, the trader seeks to profit from the net premium received, and does not want the price to fall (and the basis to narrow) such that the put is exercised.

The calculations for the breakeven point and the maximum gain and loss are shown in the following table:

BULL PUT SPREAD						
	PUTS	**PRICE**	**PREMIUM**	**PREMIUM UNITS (CENTS)**	**PRICE PER PENNY**	**COMMISSION**
	MARKET	58				
SELL	PUT CLOSEST TO MONEY	55	0.0290	2.900	$375	$1,087.50
BUY	PUT FURTHEST FROM MONEY	50	0.0120	(1.200)	$375	-$450.00
					GAIN	$637.50
MARKET PRICING SUBSEQUENT TO INCEPTION:				***PROFITABILITY:***		
	PRICE	CHANGE	VALUE	**MAXIMUM GAIN:**		
	57	0	$637.50	NET COMMISSIONS	$637.50	
	56	0	$637.50			
	55	0	$637.50	**MAXIMUM (LOSS) :**		
	54	-1	$262.50	STRIKE SPREAD x	-5	LONG - SHORT
	53.3	-0.7	$0.00	PRICE PER UNIT CHANGE	$375	
	53	-1	-$112.50	+ NET COMMISSIONS	$637.50	
	52	-1	-$487.50		-$1,237.50	
	51	-1	-$862.50	**BREAKEVEN PRICE:**		
	50	-1	-$1,237.50	SHORT STRIKE PRICE -	55	
				NET PREMIUM	1.70	
					53.30	

Bear Put

A bear put is a vertical debit spread, and the trader seeks to profit from a narrowing of the basis such that the put reaches in the money status and can be executed to offset the net premium expense. The calculations for the breakeven point and the maximum gain and loss are shown in the table below:

BEAR PUT SPREAD							
	CALLS	PRICE	PREMIUM	PREMIUM UNITS (CENTS)		PRICE PER PENNY	COMMISSION
	MARKET	58					
BUY	PUT CLOSEST TO MONEY	55	0.0250		(2.50)	$375	-$937.50
SELL	PUT FURTHEST FROM MONEY	50	0.0080		0.80	$375	$300.00
						LOSS	-$637.50

MARKET PRICING SUBSEQUENT TO INCEPTION:			PROFITABILITY:		
PRICE	CHANGE	VALUE	MAXIMUM LOSS:		
57	0	-$637.50	NET COMMISSIONS	-$637.50	
56	0	-$637.50			
55	0	-$637.50	MAXIMUM GAIN :		
54	-1	-$262.50	STRIKE SPREAD x	5	LONG - SHORT
53.3	-0.7	$0.00	PRICE PER UNIT CHANGE	$375	
53	-0.3	$112.50	+ NET COMMISSIONS	-$637.50	
52	-1	$487.50		$1,237.50	
51	-1	$862.50	BREAKEVEN PRICE:		
50	-1	$1,237.50	LONG STRIKE PRICE +	55	
			NET PREMIUM	(1.70)	
				53.30	

Bull Call

A bull call is a vertical debit spread, and the trader seeks to benefit from a narrowing of the basis such that the call reaches in the money status and can be executed to offset the net commission expense. The calculations for the breakeven point and the maximum gain and loss are shown below:

BULL CALL SPREAD						
	PUTS	PRICE	PREMIUM	PREMIUM UNITS (CENTS)	PRICE PER PENNY	COMMISSION
	MARKET	58				
BUY	CALL CLOSEST TO MONEY	65	0.0250	(2.500)	$375	-$937.50
SELL	CALL FURTHEST FROM MONEY	70	0.0080	0.800	$375	$300.00
					LOSS	-$637.50

MARKET PRICING SUBSEQUENT TO INCEPTION:			PROFITABILITY:		
PRICE	CHANGE	VALUE	MAXIMUM (LOSS):		
59	0	-$637.50	NET COMMISSIONS	-$637.50	
60	0	-$637.50			
61	0	-$637.50	MAXIMUM GAIN:		
62	0	-$637.50	STRIKE SPREAD x	5	SHORT - LONG
63	0	-$637.50	PRICE PER UNIT CHANGE	$375	
64	0	-$637.50	+ NET COMMISSIONS	-$637.50	
65	0	-$637.50		$1,237.50	
66	1	-$262.50	BREAKEVEN PRICE:		
66.7	0.7	$0.00	LONG STRIKE PRICE -	65	
67	1	$112.50	NET PREMIUM	(1.70)	
68	1	$487.50		66.70	
69	1	$862.50			
70	1	$1,237.50			

Bear Call

A bear call is a vertical credit spread, and the trader seeks to benefit from a widening of the basis. That is, the trader seeks to profit from the net premium received, and does not want the price to rise (and the basis to narrow) such that the call is exercised. The calculations for the breakeven point and the maximum gain and loss are shown in the following table:

BEAR CALL SPREAD						
	CALLS	**PRICE**	**PREMIUM**	**PREMIUM UNITS (CENTS)**	**PRICE PER PENNY**	**COMMISSION**
	MARKET	58				
SELL	CALL CLOSEST TO MONEY	65	0.0250	2.50	$375	$937.50
BUY	CALL FURTHEST FROM MONEY	70	0.0080	(0.80)	$375	-$300.00
					GAIN	$637.50
MARKET PRICING SUBSEQUENT TO INCEPTION:				***PROFITABILITY:***		
	PRICE	CHANGE	VALUE	**MAXIMUM GAIN:**		
	59	0	$637.50	NET COMMISSIONS	$637.50	
	60	0	$637.50			
	61	0	$637.50	**MAXIMUM (LOSS):**		
	62	0	$637.50	STRIKE SPREAD x	-5	SHORT - LONG
	63	0	$637.50	PRICE PER UNIT CHANGE	$375	
	64	0	$637.50	+ NET COMMISSIONS	$637.50	
	65	0	$637.50		-$1,237.50	
	66	1	$262.50	**BREAKEVEN PRICE:**		
	66.7	0.7	$0.00	SHORT STRIKE PRICE +	65	
	67	1	-$112.50	NET PREMIUM	1.70	
	68	1	-$487.50		66.70	
	69	1	-$862.50			
	70	1	-$1,237.50			

Straddle vs. Spread

A spread uses a combination of put and/or calls to establish a position. The maximum gain or loss is limited because either the put or the call will effectively establish a ceiling or a floor. In contrast, a straddle and a strangle also combine a put and a call, but both are either long or short. Therefore, the maximum gain (long position) or loss (short position) can be unlimited. A long straddle or strangle will profit from extreme price volatility in either direction. The expectation is that the price differential will offset the premium paid to establish the position. A short straddle or strangle will profit from little or no volatility, and traders seek to profit from the premium received.

Long Straddle

A trader who establishes a long straddle position expects an increase in the price volatility of the underlying commodity. The trader seeks to profit either from large upswings or downswings that are dramatic enough to offset the cost of premiums. Example:

LONG STRADDLE							
	OPTION	PRICE	QUANTITY	PREMIUM PER OPTION	OPTIONS	PREMIUM
	MARKET	52				
BUY	PUT	55	100	3.900	100	$390.00
BUY	CALL	55	100	2.900	100	$290.00
					NET EXPENSE	$680.00

MARKET PRICING SUBSEQUENT TO INCEPTION				*PROFITABILITY:*		
	PRICE	CHANGE	VALUE	**MAXIMUM GAIN:**		
	65	10	$320.00	PUT: MKT + STRIKE X QTY		UNLIMITED
	63	8	$120.00	CALL: MKT - STRIKE X QTY		
	61.80	6.8	$0.00			
	61	6	-$80.00			
	59	4	-$280.00	**MAXIMUM (LOSS) :**		
	57	2	-$480.00	NET PREMIUM		$680.00
	55	0	-$680.00			
	53	2	-$480.00			
	51	4	-$280.00	**BREAKEVEN PRICE:**	PUT	CALL
	49	6	-$80.00	NET PREMIUM EXPENSE	$680.00	$680.00
	48.20	6.8	$0.00	OPTIONS QUANTITY	100	100
	47	8	$120.00		48.20	61.80
	45	10	$320.00			

SHORT STRADDLE						
	OPTION	PRICE	QUANTITY	PREMIUM PER OPTION	OPTIONS	PREMIUM
	MARKET	52				
SELL	PUT	55	100	2.900	100	$290.00
SELL	CALL	55	100	3.900	100	$390.00
					NET INCOME	$680.00

Short Straddle

A trader who establishes a short straddle position expects little if any price volatility, which means short positions will not reach in the money status and be subject to exercise. The trader seeks to profit from the premium received. Example:

SHORT STRADDLE							
	OPTION	PRICE	QUANTITY	PREMIUM PER OPTION	OPTIONS	PREMIUM
	MARKET	52				
SELL	PUT	55	100	2.900	100	$290.00
SELL	CALL	55	100	3.900	100	$390.00
					NET INCOME	$680.00

MARKET PRICING SUBSEQUENT TO INCEPTION				PROFITABILITY:		
	PRICE	CHANGE	VALUE	MAXIMUM GAIN:		
	65	10	-$320.00	NET PREMIUM		$680.00
	63	8	-$120.00			
	61.80	6.8	$0.00			
	61	6	$80.00	MAXIMUM (LOSS) :		
	59	4	$280.00	PUT: STRIKE - MKT X QTY		UNLIMITED
	57	2	$480.00	less NET PREMIUM		
	55	0	$680.00	CALL: MKT - STRIKE X QTY		
	53	2	$480.00	less NET PREMIUM		
	51	4	$280.00			
	49	6	$80.00	BREAKEVEN PRICE:	PUT	CALL
	48.20	6.8	$0.00	NET PREMIUM EXPENSE	$680.00	$680.00
	47	8	-$120.00	OPTIONS QUANTITY	100	100
	45	10	-$320.00		48.20	61.80

Strangle vs. Straddle

A strangle operates in exactly the same way as a straddle with the exception of the strike prices of the puts and calls. In a straddle, the prices are the same for both, as the trader is indifferent to the direction of volatility. However, a strangle uses different strike prices that reflect the expectation of the trader. That is, the trader assumes a higher probability of extreme volatility for one leg of the position than for the other.

Long Strangle

The trade set-up for a long strangle is the same as the one for a long straddle with the exception of the strike prices. Example:

LONG STRANGLE						
OPTION		PRICE	QUANTITY	PREMIUM PER OPTION	OPTIONS	PREMIUM
	MARKET	35				
BUY	PUT	33	100	0.900	100	$90.00
BUY	CALL	38	100	2.900	100	$290.00
					NET EXPENSE	$380.00
MARKET PRICING SUBSEQUENT TO INCEPTION				*PROFITABILITY:*		
	PRICE	CHANGE	VALUE	**MAXIMUM GAIN:**		
	47	9	$520.00	PUT: MKT + STRIKE X QTY		UNLIMITED
	45	7	$320.00	CALL: MKT - STRIKE X QTY		
	41.8	3.8	$0.00			
	41	3	-$80.00			
	39	1	-$280.00	**MAXIMUM (LOSS) :**		
	37	0	-$380.00	NET PREMIUM		$380.00
	35	0	-$380.00			
	33	0	-$380.00			
	31	2	-$180.00	**BREAKEVEN PRICE:**	PUT	CALL
	29.2	3.8	$0.00	NET PREMIUM EXPENSE	$380.00	$380.00
	29	4	$20.00	OPTIONS QUANTITY	100	100
	27	6	$220.00		29.20	41.80
	25	8	$420.00			

Short Strangle

The trade set-up for a short strangle is the same as the one for a short straddle with the exception of the strike prices. Example:

SHORT STRANGLE						
	OPTION	PRICE	QUANTITY	PREMIUM PER OPTION	OPTIONS	PREMIUM
	MARKET	35				
SELL	PUT	33	100	0.900	100	$90.00
SELL	CALL	38	100	2.900	100	$290.00
					NET INCOME	$380.00
MARKET PRICING SUBSEQUENT TO INCEPTION				***PROFITABILITY:***		
	PRICE	CHANGE	VALUE	**MAXIMUM GAIN:**		
	47	9	-$520.00	NET PREMIUM		$380.00
	45	7	-$320.00			
	41.8	3.8	$0.00			
	41	3	$80.00	**MAXIMUM (LOSS) :**		
	39	1	$280.00	PUT: STRIKE - MKT X QTY		UNLIMITED
	37	0	$380.00	less NET PREMIUM		
	35	0	$380.00	CALL: MKT - STRIKE X QTY		
	33	0	$380.00	less NET PREMIJM		
	31	2	$180.00			
	29.2	3.8	$0.00	**BREAKEVEN PRICE:**	PUT	CALL
	29	4	-$20.00	NET PREMIUM EXPENSE	$380.00	$380.00
	27	6	-$220.00	OPTIONS QUANTITY	100	100
	25	8	-$420.00		29.20	41.80

Regulations

General Regulations

NFA

Regulatory Functions

The Commodities Exchange Act (CEA) of 1936 was created to regulate the actions of commodities traders engaged in trading futures contracts, options on futures contracts, options on physical commodities, security futures products, and some retail foreign exchange contracts. The act is administered by the Commodity Futures Trading Commission (CFTC). Section 17 of the CEA provides for the registration of industry self-regulating organizations with the CFTC, which play in role in regulating the actions of their members. The National Futures Association (NFA) is the only such organization currently registered, and acts on behalf of the CFTC. The NFA is responsible for the following regulatory functions:

- auditing and surveillance of NFA members for the purpose of enforcing and ensuring compliance with NFA financial requirements
- establishment and enforcement of rules and standards to ensure customer protection
- administration and maintenance of an arbitration process to adjudicate disputes arising from futures and foreign exchange transactions
- determination of fitness of applicants for membership and review of continuing membership for existing members

Roles of Individuals or Firms Required to Be Registered

In general, any individual or firm acting in a role in which customer contact occurs for the purposes of receiving orders for futures and option contracts, executing orders for futures and option contracts, processing payments, and accounting for trading activities on behalf of customers is required to be registered with the National Futures Association (NFA). These roles include:

- futures commission merchant
- introducing broker
- commodity trading advisor
- commodity pool operator
- floor broker
- floor trader
- associated person

Floor broker vs. floor trader: A floor trader is an individual who conducts floor trading activities, but also acts on behalf of his or her own account. Although floor traders do not execute orders on behalf of customers, they are subject to the same registration requirements as floor brokers [National Futures Association (NFA) Registration Rule 205]. That is, they must be registered through the NFA, although they do not need to be actual members of the NFA.

Associated person: An associated person is an individual who is employed by an FCM [or associated with an introducing broker (IB), a commodity trading advisor (CTA), or a commodity pool operator (CPO)] and involved in any capacity with the solicitation or acceptance of customer orders. An associated person (AP) must be sponsored for registration by an FCM or other registrant (such as an IB, a CTA, or a CPO). The AP must provide certification of such sponsorship to the National

Futures Association (NFA). A prospective AP must also satisfy the proficiency requirements of the NFA by achieving a satisfactory score on the Series 3 exam. The registration of an AP will remain valid only while he or she is employed by the sponsor.

Generally, all individuals who have contact with customers for the purpose of securing orders and all individuals in the related supervisory chain must register as associated persons (APs) with the National Futures Association (NFA). The exceptions to the AP registration requirement are as follows:

- The individual is already registered with the National Futures Association (NFA) as either a futures commission merchant (FCM), an introducing broker (IB), or a floor broker (FB).
- The individual is already registered as a commodity pool operator (CPO) in association with a CPO, unless he or she is already registered with the National Association of Securities Dealers (NASD) and futures activity is specific to the CPO only.
- The individual is already registered as a commodity trading advisor (CTA) in association with a CTA.

Rule 401

Rule 401 states that any National Futures Association (NFA) applicant acting in the following roles is required to demonstrate proficiency via a satisfactory score on the Series 3 proficiency exam:

- futures commission merchant (FCM)
- retail foreign exchange dealer (RFED)
- introducing broker (IB)
- commodity pool operator (CPO)
- commodity trading advisor (CTA)
- leverage transaction merchant (LTM)
- any associated person (AP) associated with the above roles

Exemption of CPO

A CPO may be exempt from NFA registration if certain characteristics of the pool fall below certain size and operational thresholds. For example, if a CPO's compensation is limited to cover his operating expenses, if the CPO operates only one pool, and if the pool is not advertised, then the CPO may be exempt. Another way a CPO may be exempt is if none of the pools he operates has more than 15 participants and if the total aggregate gross capital contributions for his managed pools do not exceed $400,000.

Individuals Who Provide Trading Advice

Generally speaking, an individual qualifies as a CTA if advice is provided either directly or indirectly. However, NFA registration rules provide a registration requirement exemption if the advice provided is not specifically tailored to the individual account of a customer. Examples would include publications such as books and periodicals, which present the same advice to all readers. Exemptions also exist for those whose advisory services are an incidental part of their trade or business.

These exempt individuals include:

- individuals who advise no more than 15 people, and do not present themselves to the public as a CTA
- individuals engaged in a business subject to state regulation (such as an insurance company)
- individuals engaged in the business of cash markets, such as dealers, brokers, or sellers
- individuals engaged in various other professions specifically defined by the CEA

Registration as an IB

Generally speaking, a CTA also acting as an IB is required to register as an IB unless one of two conditions is present:

- The accounts under management are a result of a power of attorney. OR
- Compensation is not collected on a fee per trade basis.

IB and FCM

An IB cannot accept customer funds, and therefore requires the services of an FCM. The FCM may act either in a service provider capacity, where the IB remains independent, or in a guarantor capacity. An IB acting under a guaranty agreement with an FCM is required to process all customer activity through the guarantor FCM. An independent IB is not restricted to using a specific FCM to process customer account activity. Regulations prevent an IB from accepting customer funds with the exception of checks made payable to a futures commission merchant (FCM). Therefore, an IB must register as an FCM in order to accept customer payments. An IB that registers as an FCM is subject to a higher threshold with respect to minimum capital and reporting requirements.

CEA

Generally, any individual or firm that wants to trade futures must register with the National Futures Association (NFA), unless certain exemptions apply. The governing statute to which NFA rules must conform is the Commodity Exchange Act (CEA). These rules must also comply with the regulations of the Commodity Futures Trading Commission (CFTC).

NFA Audit

NFA audits are intended to accomplish the following:

- Ascertain whether the record keeping program is in compliance with the applicable rules of the NFA and the regulations of the Commodity Futures Trading Commission (CFTC).
- Ensure that the member is in compliance with NFA rules regarding sales practices (Rules 2-2, 2-4, and 2-29).

NFA Membership Requirements

In 1978, legislation that amended the Commodity Exchange Act (CEA) was passed. It provided for mandatory membership in at least one futures association that would act in a regulatory capacity on behalf of the Commodity Futures Trading Commission (CFTC). Since the National Futures Association (NFA) is the only such registered futures association, the legislation effectively made NFA membership mandatory.

The legislation, CFTC Regulation 170.15, applied only to futures commission merchants (FCMs). Article VI of the NFA Articles of Incorporation expanded the membership requirement to include the following futures professionals:

- commodity pool operator (CPO)
- commodity trading advisor (CTA)
- introducing broker (IB)
- leverage transaction merchant (LTM)

NFA by-law 1101 expressly prohibits any NFA member from accepting futures orders from any individuals or firms (except direct customers) that are not also members of the NFA.

NFA Member and NFA Registrant

Any person registered with the Commodity Futures Trading Commission (CFTC) to conduct futures trading is eligible for membership in the NFA. In addition, any contract market (such as the CBOT, the CME, etc.) and any individual specifically qualified by a CFTC rule is eligible for membership. In addition, the following professionals are required by statute to become members of the NFA:

- futures transaction merchant (FCM)
- commodity pool operator (CPO)
- commodity trading advisor (CTA)
- introducing broker (IB)
- leverage transaction merchant (LTM)

In addition to the professions listed above, registration (but not membership) is required for the following professionals:

- floor broker (FB)
- floor trader (FT)
- associated person (AP)

Note that FBs and FTs are regulated by the exchange with which trading privileges are maintained.

Requirements for AP Trading in Discretionary Account of Customer

An AP is required to have been continuously registered with the NFA for a minimum of two years while concurrently operating in the capacity of an AP in order to trade in the discretionary account of a customer. The exception is if the AP is already registered as a CTA. The NFA has the discretion to waive the experience requirement based upon evidence of equivalent experience.

Customer Information Required to Establish Trading Account

National Futures Association (NFA) Compliance Rule 2-30 (the know your customer rule) requires that the risks of futures trading be disclosed to customers before a trading account is opened. The minimum information that must be provided by customers in order to establish a trading account is as follows:

- the name, address, and principal occupation or business of the customer
- the current estimated annual income and net worth of the customer (if the customer is an individual)

- the customer's net worth or net assets and current estimated annual income; or, if current income is not available, the customer's annual income for the previous year (if the customer is not an individual)
- the approximate age and/or date of birth of the customer (if the customer is an individual)
- an indication of the previous investment and futures trading experience of the customer
- other information considered to be reasonable and appropriate by the member or associate in order to appropriately disclose the risks of futures trading to the customer

The futures commission merchant (FCM) member who is responsible for an individual customer's account is required to contact the customer at least annually to verify that the information previously obtained from the customer is still accurate. The FCM member must also give the customer an opportunity to correct or add any necessary account information.

The responsible FCM member must determine whether an additional risk disclosure must be provided to the customer whenever he or she is notified of material changes to customer information.

Customer Information Provided by NFA Member Who Is Not a FINRA Member

Information about the customer provided by a National Futures Association (NFA) member who is not also registered as a member of the Financial Industry Regulatory Authority (FINRA) and intends to trade security-based futures on behalf of a customer include the following details:

- The intent of the customer to engage in either hedging or speculation
- The employment status of the customer (name of employer, self-employed, retired, etc.)
- The estimated net worth of the customer (cash, securities, properties, other)
- The marital status of the customer and the number of dependents
- Other information that the member or associate considers reasonable and relevant, and will allow the member or associate to provide appropriate recommendations to the customer

Compliance Rule 2-8

Once a trade has been executed in a discretionary account, additional steps are required to ensure proper compliance with Compliance Rule 2-8 of the National Futures Association (NFA). NFA Rule 2-8 requires that all trading in discretionary accounts be reviewed by a principal of the member in order to ensure the following:

- A partner, officer, director, branch office manager, or supervisory employee of the member regularly reviews discretionary trading activity, and a designated security futures principal regularly reviews discretionary security futures trading.
- A written record that such review procedures were performed by a partner, officer, director, branch office manager, supervisory employee, or designated security futures principal is created.

Foreign Futures/Options

Compliance Rule 2-8 states, in part, that an NFA member or associate cannot exercise discretion with regard to foreign futures or foreign options transactions on behalf of a customer unless the customer or account controller has specifically given written authorization for the member or associate to exercise such discretion. As with all transactions, written authorization should be provided in the form of a power of attorney or other such instrument.

Compliance with CFTC and Bank Secrecy Act and the Department of the Treasury

The minimum program requirements intended to ensure member compliance with Commodity Futures Trading Commission (CFTC) regulations and the anti-money laundering regulations of the Bank Secrecy Act and the Department of the Treasury include the following:

- the establishment and implementation of reasonably designed policies, procedures, and internal controls that are sufficient to ensure compliance with the applicable provisions of the Bank Secrecy Act and implementing regulations
- the establishment of an independent testing compliance program administered by a member or a similarly qualified outside party
- the designation and assignment of an individual or individuals who will assume responsibility for the implementation and monitoring of daily operations and internal program controls
- the establishment of a continuous training program for appropriate personnel

Daily Reporting Requirements

The CFTC and the exchanges require daily reporting from futures commission merchants (FCM) and clearing members in all so-called reportable positions. Any single trader that exceeds certain thresholds set by either the CFTC or the exchange regarding the net long or short position in a single futures or option (or all futures or options for a single commodity) is deemed to be in a reportable position. The purpose of the disclosure is to identify and thus preclude any attempts by a trader to accumulate a position sufficiently large to enable market control and price manipulation of a commodity futures or option.

The data elements that must be included in the daily reports to the CFTC include the following:

- the net position (long or short) of each futures contract, as well as the strike price and expiration date of each put or call option
- the gross position (long or short) of each futures contract, as well as the strike price and expiration date of each put or call option if:
  - Such positions are reported to the exchange on a gross basis. OR
  - The account is held jointly with multiple persons. OR
  - Multiple accounts are controlled by a single trader.

Large Trader Reporting Requirements of the CFTC

The term large trader signifies that the limit on positions has been reached, which triggers a reportable event. A futures commission merchant (FCM), clearing member, or foreign broker must include a special account identification report containing background information for each large trader in his or her daily report. In addition, each large trader may be asked to provide additional information to the CFTC upon request, such as:

- name, address, and principal business or occupation for the reporting trader and each person with control over such a trader
- commercial business activity and registration status with the CFTC
- disclosure of other accounts with a financial interest of not less than 10%
- names and locations of any FCM and/or foreign broker holding futures accounts for the reporting trader

Special Call Provision

A special call is used by the CFTC to obtain information from registered individuals or entities for specific purposes. Examples of such special call information include the following:

- information regarding persons who exercise control over the trading in a customer account
- information regarding open contracts containing specific futures or options positions owned or controlled by traders
- information on selected special open contracts of various traders or clearing members identified by the CFTC

Exemption from Position Reporting Limits

A speculative position limit sets the maximum value a single trader can hold in a single futures or option contract, regardless of whether the position is net short or net long. Hedge positions which conform to the structure defined by the Commodity Futures Trading Commission (CFTC) are generally exempt from position reporting limits. While the defined structure can be quite specific, the general requirements for a qualifying hedge are that the hedge:

- represents a substitute for transactions made or to be made, or for positions taken or to be taken at a later time in a physical marketing channel
- is economically appropriate for the purpose of reducing risk related to the conduct and management of a commercial enterprise
- arises from the potential change of one or several underlying assets

Speculative Position Limits and Position Accountability Limits

Speculative position limits represent the maximum position of combined futures and options (either net long or net short) that may be held by any single trader or group of traders acting in concert. CFTC regulations currently apply such limits to grains, the soybean complex, and cotton. Exchanges may extend the limits to other commodities.

Position accountability limits permit traders to accumulate positions that exceed the limitation amounts in exchange for on-demand reporting of such positions as requested by the CFTC and/or the exchange.

FCM/IB Regulations

Responsibilities of FCM That Acts as Guarantor for IB

Any FCM that enters into a guaranty agreement with an IB using the required guaranty form guarantees the performance of the IB, and shall be jointly and severally liable for all obligations of the IB under the Commodity Exchange Act (CEA). In addition, National Futures Association (NFA) Compliance Rule 2-23 states that a guarantor FCM assumes responsibility for acts and omissions of the member IB that are in violation of NFA requirements and occur during the term of the guaranty agreement. In this situation, the guarantor FCM is subject to the same disciplinary action as the IB.

Acceptance of Customer Funds by IB

An IB is required to use the services of an associated futures commission merchant (FCM) for receipt of all customer funds, including securities and property. The sole exception is receiving checks from a customer that are made payable to an FCM. In this situation, the IB must be acting as a conduit for bank deposit or delivery.

Minimum Capital Levels Required by NFA for Independent IB vs. Guaranteed IB

An independent IB is required to maintain adjusted net capital in the amount of the greater of:

- $45,000
- if less than $1 million, $6,000 for each remote operation
- if less than $1 million, $3,000 for each sponsored associated person

The capital requirements for a guaranteed IB are included as part of the guarantor futures commission merchant (FCM) requirements.

NFA Capital Requirements for FCM

An FCM is required to maintain adjusted net capital in the amount of the greater of:

- $1 million
- if less than $2 million, $6,000 for each remote operation (including IBs)
- if less than $2 million, $3,000 for each sponsored associated person (AP), including any AP of an IB
- 8% of the total risk margin for all customer account positions, plus 8% of the total risk margin for all FCM proprietary positions

Capital Requirements for FCM That Guarantees IB

A futures commission merchant (FCM) that wishes to affiliate with an introducing broker via a guaranty agreement is subject to additional minimum capital requirements. The minimum capital requirements for an FCM that guarantees an IB are as follows:

- 150% of the capital required for a non-guaranty FCM
- if less than $2 million, $9,000 for each remote location operated, including each guaranteed IB
- if less than $2 million, $4,500 for each sponsored AP, including each guaranteed AP
- for securities dealers, the amount required by the SEC
- 110% of the following calculated value: 8% of the total risk margin for all customer account positions plus 8% of the total risk margin for all FCM proprietary positions

Financial Reporting Requirements for FCMs and Independent IBs

Both FCMs and independent IBs are subject to minimum capital requirements and, as such, are subject to the financial reporting requirements listed below. These NFA Recordkeeping Rule 2-10 requirements are above and beyond those that are applicable to all NFA members.

- Financial reports required to be filed with the Commodity Futures Trading Commission (CFTC) and/or the NFA must be prepared in English, must use U.S. dollars, and must comply with U.S. accounting standards.
- A general ledger must be maintained in English, and must use U.S. dollars.

Requirements for Margins Expressed in Foreign Currencies

Initial and maintenance margin deposit levels required of customers of both futures commodity merchants (FCMs) and introducing brokers (IBs) are determined by the exchange, and are usually expressed in U.S. dollars. An FCM or an IB may accept foreign currency margin deposits if a subordination agreement is in place with the owner of the account and the FCM or IB ascertains that the rules of the exchange allow the use of such instruments.

Customer Complaints

A valid customer complaint must involve a registered trading professional, and must allege one or more violations of either the Commodities Exchange Act (CEA) or the regulations of the Commodity Futures Trading Commission (CFTC). Actions subject to complaint include the following:

- fraud, including false or misleading statements
- breach of fiduciary duty
- unauthorized trading
- misappropriation or diversion of funds
- churning (excessive trading)
- wrongful liquidation of an account
- failure to supervise
- nondisclosure

The Commodity Futures Trading Commission's (CFTC) reparations program is designed to adjudicate customer complaints against registered professionals. The three types of proceedings that are available to claimants are as follows:

- Voluntary – Both the claimant and the respondent agree to provide written submissions to a judgment officer, who will make a decision. Any decisions made are final, and cannot be appealed.
- Summary – This type of proceeding is used in cases where claims do not exceed $30,000 and the voluntary procedure is not selected. The claimant provides written submissions to a judgment officer, who can convene an oral hearing and render a judgment at his or her discretion. The decision may be appealed.
- Formal – This type of proceeding is used in cases where claims exceed $30,000 and the voluntary procedure is not selected. The claimant provides written submissions to a judgment officer, who may convene a formal in-person hearing and render a judgment at his or her discretion. The decision may be appealed.

In order to be considered for the CFTC reparations program, a complaint must meet the following criteria:

- There must be attestation that any losses claimed as damages are the result of the activities described in the complaint.
- The respondents named in the complaint committed the alleged activities.
- The alleged activities committed by the respondents appear to be in violation of the Commodity Exchange Act (CEA) or the regulations of the CFTC.

Documentation Upon Receipt of Customer Order

An FCM who receives a customer order that is subject to margin requirements must immediately document the receipt of the order. This documentation must include certain basic information:

- customer account identification
- unique order number
- date and time (to the nearest minute) when the order was received

NFA Rule 2-29

In general, NFA Rule 2-29 regarding communication with the public prohibits information which is fraudulent or deceitful, is part of a high-pressure approach, and/or states that futures trading is appropriate for all persons. Promotional materials are prohibited from including content that:

- is likely to deceive the public
- contains any material misstatement of fact or purposely omits any fact, which renders the promotional material misleading
- mentions the possibility of profit without an equally prominent statement of the risk of loss
- makes reference to actual past trading profits without a disclaimer that such results are not necessarily indicative of future results
- includes any specific numerical or statistical information regarding the past financial performance and rate of return of any actual accounts, unless such information meets specific requirements and regulations set by the CFTC
- includes any testimonial that does not prominently feature displayed statements indicating that the testimonial is neither indicative of future performance nor provided in exchange for compensation, and that the testimonial is not representative of all reasonably comparable accounts

CPO/CTA

CFTC Regulation 4.24.i

CFTC Regulation 4.24.i regarding commodity pool operators (CPOs) requires disclosure of specific fees incurred by the pool. The fees that must be disclosed by a CPO include the following:

- management fees
- brokerage fees and commissions
- trading advice fees and commissions
- collective investment fees and expenses
- incentive fees
- allocations
- commissions for solicitation
- professional, general, and administrative expenses
- organizational and offering expenses
- clearance fees
- fees for principal protected pools
- bid/ask spread fees

CFTC Regulation 4.25.b

According to Commodity Futures Trading Commission (CFTC) Regulation 4.25.b, performance disclosure is mandatory for a commodity pool operator (CPO) when:

- The pool has a minimum of three years of trading history.
- No less than 75% of the contributions to the pool originated from unaffiliated investors.

Regulation 4.24 Disclosure Statements

Regulation 4.24 of the Commodity Futures Trading Commission (CFTC) requires a commodity pool operator (CPO) to complete two types of disclosure statements. The two types of disclosure statements required from a CPO are as follows:

- Cautionary statement – This is a statement with specific language outlined in the CFTC regulations. The statement indicates that the CFTC makes no representation about the adequacy of the disclosure.
- Risk disclosure statement – This is a detailed statement with specific language outlined in the CFTC regulations. The statement concerns the inherent risks of futures transactions.

CFTC Regulation 4.24.h

Commodity Futures Trading Commission (CFTC) Regulation 4.24.h requires disclosure of the commodity pool operator's (CPO) investment program and the use of proceeds. Such disclosure includes the types of commodities that the pool will trade and the trading and investment programs and policies that will be followed. The CPO investment program disclosure must also include the following:

- the commodity trading advisors (CTAs) that will be employed and the nature and operation of the proposed trading program
- the amount of assets that will be held in segregation in order to fulfill the margin requirements of the pool

CFTC Regulation 4.24.f

Commodity Futures Trading Commission (CFTC) Regulation 4.24.f requires a five-year business background for certain commodity pool operator (CPO) principals, including each commodity trading advisor (CTA) and investee pool operator. In addition to each CTA and investee pool operator, the CPO must disclose:

- any pool trading manager
- operators of each major investee pool
- each and every principal who participates in the decision-making process or supervises those who do

CFTC Regulation 4.24.j

Commodity Futures Trading Commission (CFTC) Regulation 4.24.j requires actual or perceived conflicts of interest on the part of certain principals of a commodity pool operator (CPO) to be disclosed. The principals that must be disclosed by the CPO include the following:

- commodity pool operators
- pool trading managers
- commodity trading advisors
- CPOs of any major investee pool
- any other persons providing services to the pool

CFTC Regulation 4.34.j

Commodity Futures Trading Commission (CFTC) Regulation 4.34.j regarding the disclosure of perceived conflicts of interest on the part of certain principals of commodity trading advisors (CTAs) is similar to the disclosure rules for commodity pool operators (CPOs). The following are the two principal roles not included in the CPO requirements:

- CPOs must disclose each CTA that is advising a pool.
- CTAs must disclose futures commission merchants (FCMs) and introducing brokers, as well as their supervisors.

In addition to CTAs, the following principals must disclose any real or perceived conflicts of interest:

- any futures commission merchant (FCM)
- any retail foreign exchange dealer (RFED)
- any introducing broker (IB)

CFTC Regulation 4.35

The regulation requires that performance information be disclosed for the most recent five years before the current one, or for inception to present, whichever is the lesser time period. Information for the current year to date must also be provided. Commodity Futures Trading Commission (CFTC) Regulation 4.35 requires two types of disclosure statements from a commodity trading advisor (CTA). The disclosure statements required from a CTA are the same ones required from a commodity pool operator. They are described below:

- Cautionary statement – This is a statement with specific language outlined in the CFTC regulations. The statement indicates that the CFTC makes no representation about the adequacy of the disclosure.
- Risk disclosure statement – This is a detailed statement with specific language outlined in the CFTC regulations. The statement concerns the inherent risks of futures transactions.

CFTC Regulation 4.34.f

Any individual responsible for supervising a CTA must also provide a five-year business background. Supervisors include all individuals in the supervisory or reporting chain of command.

Alternative Trades

Commodity pool operators (CPOs) and/or commodity trading advisors (CTAs) are required to maintain written records on transactions that can be classified as alternative trades. Alternative trades include the following two types of transactions:

- A block trade is a single, large volume transaction that is negotiated ex-pit (outside of an exchange), and then executed on the floor of an exchange. Such transactions are subject to review and cancellation at the discretion of the Commodity Futures Trading Commission (CFTC).
- A bunched order is a single order executed on behalf of multiple customers.

Rule 2-29 and Related Rules

National Futures Association (NFA) Rule 2-29 regarding promotional materials is one of a number of such rules intended to codify the Commodity Exchange Act (CEA) requirement to "establish minimum standards governing the sales practices of its members" and other associated persons. It is intended to augment other related compliance rules. These other related rules are as follows:

- Rule 2-14 regulates the advertising of commodity pool operators (CPOs) and commodity trading advisors (CTAs).
- Rule 2-2 applies to all members and associated persons (AP). It is concerned with fraud and deceit, and essentially requires that high ethical standards related to customer relationships be met.
- Rule 2-4 also applies to all members and associated persons (AP). It is concerned with just and equitable principles of trade, and requires that high commercial honor standards be met.

Arbitration Procedures

Arbitrable Disputes

In general, arbitration procedures are mandatory in situations where there is a dispute between a National Futures Association (NFA) member and a customer. In order for a dispute brought forth by a customer against a member or member associate to be arbitrable, the following three conditions must be met:

- The customer cannot be a futures commission merchant (FCM), a floor broker (FB), an NFA member, or an associated person (AP).
- The nexus of the dispute cannot involve cash market transactions that do not have a direct relationship to a futures transaction.
- The respondent NFA member or associate must be a futures commission merchant (FCM), a retail foreign exchange dealer (RFED), an introducing broker (IB), a commodity pool operator (CPO), a commodity trading advisor (CTA), or a leverage transaction merchant (LTM).

An arbitration claim or notice of intent to arbitrate must be filed with the NFA within two years of the date on which the claimant became aware or should have become aware that an arbitrable dispute existed.

Third Party Claim

A third party claim (filed by a respondent against a party not subject to the proceedings) may be filed if the claim has arisen out of an act or a transaction that is the subject of the arbitration claim.

Arbitration Panel

The secretary of the National Futures Association (NFA) is responsible for appointing an arbitration panel to adjudicate dispute proceedings. Arbitration panel members must be NFA members or individuals associated with NFA members. The criteria for determining the size of an arbitration panel are as follows:

- For claims not greater than $100,000, the panel consists of a single panel member.
- For claims greater than $100,000, the panel consists of three panel members.
- For claims between $50,000 and not more than $100,000, an additional two members may be appointed upon the request of all parties involved.

Filing and Answer to a Claim

Once an arbitration claim has been filed, the National Futures Association (NFA) will initiate the proceedings by notifying each person named on the claim as a respondent. Answers must be filed by the respondent within the time periods below:

- for claims not exceeding $50,000, 20 days from the date of service of the claim by the NFA
- for claims greater than $50,000 but not exceeding $100,000, 45 days from the date of service of the claim by the NFA
- for claims greater than $100,000, 45 days from the date of service of the claim by the NFA

Individuals Authorized to Act as Counsel

Parties to an arbitration proceeding held before the National Futures Association (NFA) are entitled to be assisted by counsel. Any party to such a dispute may be represented by:

- an attorney
- a non-compensated family member who has no vested interest in the outcome of the dispute
- an officer, partner, or employee of the party

Hearing Plan

During the pre-hearing phase of an arbitration proceeding held before the National Futures Association (NFA), the parties are expected to cooperate by exchanging all relevant documents and jointly contributing to the preparation of a hearing plan. A hearing plan is a document that summarizes each claim, each answer to a claim, and each reply to an answer. The document also includes:

- the factual and legal issues pertaining to the dispute
- a list of witnesses and exhibits that will be presented at the hearing

Dismissal of a Claim

A panel may dismiss a claim either of its own initiative or at the request of one or both of the parties if it determines that the claim is not a proper subject for NFA arbitration. This determination is made at the panel's discretion.

Summary Hearing

An arbitration panel hearing is scheduled by the secretary of the National Futures Association (NFA). At the designated time, the parties are afforded the opportunity to appear, testify, and present evidence before the panel. A hearing can be a summary hearing (conducted using written material only) in the following three circumstances. The secretary of the panel must also agree to conduct a summary hearing.

- The amount of the claims in aggregate does not exceed $25,000.
- The amount of the claims in aggregate is greater than $25,000, but does not exceed $50,000, and one of the parties requests an oral hearing.
- Both parties request a summary hearing and the panel agrees to waive an oral hearing.

Modification of Award

Generally, decisions by the arbitration panel of the National Futures Association (NFA) and any related awards are considered to be final and binding on the parties. Typically, the parties do not have a right to appeal. After the final judgment, an award may be modified in the following circumstances when a written request is made by one of the parties within 20 days of the date of service of the award:

- The award was based on a material calculation error or on an improper description of any person, thing, or property relevant to the award.
- The award was based on a matter not properly referred to the panel.
- The award is imperfect in matter of form.

Arbitration Costs Against Respondent

Arbitration costs required by the National Futures Association (NFA) are the responsibility of the claimant. A panel may assess reasonable and necessary expenses against a respondent if the panel finds the respondent engaged in willful acts of bad faith or presented a frivolous defense. Attorney fees may also be assessed in situations where this is legally permitted.

Disciplinary Proceedings

When disputes are submitted to arbitration or mediation, the NFA retains the right to initiate a disciplinary proceeding at its discretion.

NFA Disciplinary Procedures

Requirements of Compliance Director in Investigation

National Futures Association (NFA) Compliance Rule 2-9 requires that all members exercise an appropriate level of supervision over employees and agents. Necessary complaints must be submitted to the compliance director of the NFA Business Conduct Committee (BCC). According to Compliance Rule 3-2, in response to an investigation, the compliance director is required to issue a written report to the BCC that includes the following information:

- the reason for the initiation of the investigation
- a summary of the complaint, if a complaint was created
- the relevant facts of the investigation
- a recommendation for the BCC to proceed further (if applicable)

BCC Actions

Once the compliance director issues a completed report to the Business Compliance Committee (BCC) of the National Futures Association (NFA) no later than four months from the date of the inception of the investigation, within 30 days of receiving the report from the compliance director, the BCC must decide between two courses of action:

- If there is no reasonable basis to assume a violation has occurred, the BCC must close the matter.
- If there is reason to believe that a violation has occurred, the BCC must issue a formal written and dated complaint.

Warning Letter

Upon completion of an investigation by the compliance director, the BCC of the National Futures Association (NFA) may, at the recommendation of the compliance director, issue a warning letter if there is no reason to believe that a violation has occurred.

Complaint Information

If, as the result of an investigation, the Business Conduct Committee (BCC) of the National Futures Association (NFA) finds that a rule has been violated and a written and dated complaint is warranted, a complaint issued by the BCC must include the following information:

- each NFA violation alleged to have occurred, or each NFA violation that, but for the complaint, would have occurred
- each act or omission which precipitated the violation

Settlement Proposal

National Futures Association (NFA) members subject to a formal complaint by the BCC are entitled to a hearing before a board comprised of members of the NFA Hearing Committee. If a respondent desires a settlement, a settlement may be submitted to the hearing panel at any time prior to the appointment of a hearing panel chairman.

Appeal by Respondent

If the National Futures Association (NFA) arbitration hearing panel issues a decision against a respondent, a respondent may file a written notice of appeal with the National Futures Association (NFA) within 15 days of the date on which the hearing panel issued its decision. The respondent must describe the elements of the decision that are the subject of the appeal, and must outline any request to personally appear before the panel.

MRA

A member responsibility action (MRA) is a summary action that may be taken by the president of the NFA in circumstances where an NFA member is deemed to pose a risk to the operations of the market, as well as to customers and other NFA members. With the agreement of the NFA's Board of Directors or the Executive Committee of the NFA, the president may take whatever steps are necessary to avoid adverse impacts.

Summary Actions Taken Against NFA Member Prior to Hearing

With the agreement of the NFA's Board of Directors or the Executive Committee of the NFA, the president of the NFA may suspend the membership of the member or associate, restrict the operations of the member or associate (including his or her ability to associate with other members), or demand immediate remedial action by the member prior to a hearing.

Penalties

The penalties that may be imposed upon a violating member include:

- expulsion from the NFA or suspension for a specified time period
- suspension from association with another NFA member
- censure or reprimand
- a fine not exceeding $250,000 per violation
- an order to cease and desist
- any other penalty not inconsistent with this rule

CFTC Commodity Exchange Act Enforcement

Enforcement of CEA

Enforcement of the Commodities Exchange Act (CEA) is the responsibility of the Division of Enforcement of the Commodity Futures Trading Commission (CFTC). The Division of Enforcement may take enforcement action against individuals in the following situations:

- violations of laws by individuals involved with futures trading on domestic exchanges
- improperly marketed futures products in furtherance of Ponzi schemes
- manipulative or deceptive schemes by individuals trading futures contracts
- usage of disruptive trading practices

Administrative Sanctions

Individuals found to be in violation of the Commodities Exchange Act (CEA) and/or the regulations of the CFTC may be subject to the following sanctions:

- civil monetary penalties
- suspension, denial, revocation, or restriction of trading privileges
- orders of restitution
- appointment of receiver
- freeze of assets
- disgorgement of ill-gotten gains

Criminal Violations

All criminal actions are referred to the Department of Justice for investigation and prosecution.

Series 3 Practice Test

1. What is excessive trading that results in increased commissions for the broker while providing no benefit to the customer called?

   a. Arbitrage
   b. Charting
   c. Churning
   d. Bidding

2. What is the tendency for prices of physical commodities and futures to approach one another, usually during the delivery month?

   a. Divergence
   b. Convergence
   c. Arbitrage
   d. Bucketing

3. What is an individual who solicits orders, customers, or customer funds on behalf of a futures commission merchant, an introducing broker, a commodity trading advisor, or a commodity pool operator and is registered with the Commodity Futures Trading Commission called?

   a. Associated person
   b. Floor broker
   c. Floor trader
   d. Scalper

4. Who is the individual who executes orders on the trading floor of an exchange for any other person?

   a. Introducing broker
   b. Scalper
   c. Floor broker
   d. Floor trader

5. What is a trader who trades for small, short-term profits during one trading session and rarely holds a position overnight?

   a. Day trader
   b. Position trader
   c. Floor trader
   d. Scalper

6. What is the smallest increment of a price movement for a futures contract called?

   a. Spot
   b. Spread
   c. Short
   d. Tick

7. An option writer can also be referred to as an option seller.

   a. True
   b. False

8. The strike price is the price that the holder of an option pays and the writer of an option receives for the rights conveyed by the option.

a. True
b. False

9. A call option is in the money if the current market value of the underlying security is above the exercise price of the option.

a. True
b. False

10. Intrinsic value is the amount, if any, that an option is in the money.

a. True
b. False

11. If the exercise price of a put is above the current market value of the underlying security, it is considered to be out of the money.

a. True
b. False

12. When computing margin calls, option values of all options contracts are not allowed to meet an account's total risk margin requirement.

a. True
b. False

13. What is a performance bond also referred to as?

a. Future
b. Option
c. Margin
d. Hedge

14. Which of the following is not specified in a futures contract?

a. The item being bought and sold
b. The strike price
c. The contract month
d. The manner of settlement

15. What is a feature of futures trading whose risks are the mirror image of its potential benefits?

a. Leverage
b. Hedging
c. Margin
d. Speculation

16. What is establishing a position in the futures market that is equal and opposite to a position in the cash market called?

a. Leveraging
b. Speculating
c. Bucketing
d. Hedging

17. How often are gains and losses credited or debited to the accounts of buyers and sellers of futures contracts?

a. Hourly
b. Daily
c. Weekly
d. Monthly

18. What is the minimum margin requirement for security futures set by law?

a. 20% of the contract value
b. 25% of the contract value
c. 30% of the contract value
d. 35% of the contract value

19. What is the initial margin requirement on the purchase of a futures contract worth $5,000?

a. $500
b. $750
c. $1,000
d. $1,500

20. What is it called when an investor takes a long position in a futures contract of one maturity and a short position in a contract on the same commodity with a different maturity?

a. Straddle
b. Option
c. Hedge
d. Spread

21. An investor purchased 5 September wheat futures contracts at 7.35. The contract is trending up in price, peaking at 9.85. The investor, going forward, would like to sell the contracts and maximize his profit but is concerned that the price will start trading lower, possibly reaching 7.50. Which of the following orders should he enter to protect and maximize profit?

a. Buy 5 September wheat futures at 7.00 stop.
b. Sell 5 September wheat futures at 7.25 stop.
c. Sell 5 September wheat futures at 8.25 stop.
d. Sell 5 September wheat futures at 9.25 stop.

22. An investor purchased 17 April corn futures contracts at 14.50. At which of the following prices will this investor be able to sell his 17 April corn futures contracts while maximizing the profit on the transaction?

a. 14.00
b. 15.25
c. 14.25
d. 15.75

23. In the futures industry, *margin* refers to a partial payment for the contract being purchased.

a. True
b. False

24. Buyers of futures contracts have the same ownership interests or voting rights and receive the same dividends as stock owners.

a. True
b. False

25. Failure to meet a margin call within the time period allowed may result in the broker liquidating a customer's open futures positions at the current market price without prior notice.

a. True
b. False

26. An investor establishes a short position by selling 9 May silver futures contracts at 57.25. At which of the following prices will this investor be able to purchase 9 May silver contracts to cover the short position while still maximizing profit?

a. 57.00
b. 57.75
c. 55.75
d. 58.25

27. What is a request for additional margin?

a. Margin call
b. Margin maintenance
c. Initial margin
d. Margin spread

28. If the initial margin required to buy or sell a futures contract is $5,000 and the maintenance margin requirement is $4,000, what is the amount of the margin call if losses on open positions reduce the funds remaining in the account to $3,000?

a. $1,000
b. $2,000
c. $4,000
d. $5,000

29. In what year did futures contracts begin trading in the United States?

a. 1965
b. 1892
c. 1982
d. 1865

30. If an S&P 500 index futures contract is currently trading at a price of 145–00, what is the intrinsic value of a call option conveying the right to purchase that futures contract at a strike price of 135–00?

a. $5,000
b. $10,000
c. $500
d. $1,000

31. An investor is short 1 October wheat 600 call at 3. What will be the maximum gain, maximum loss, and breakeven on this position?

a. The maximum gain is $3, maximum loss is unlimited, and breakeven is $600.
b. The maximum gain is unlimited, maximum loss is $300, and breakeven is $603.
c. The maximum gain is $300, maximum loss is unlimited, and breakeven is $603.
d. The maximum gain is $300, maximum loss is unlimited, and breakeven is $600.

32. Cash corn is trading at $5.85 per bushel. There's a monthly storage fee of $0.11 per bushel and a monthly insurance cost per bushel of $0.03. Given these parameters, what would be the total cost per bushel to buy the corn and hold onto it for four months?

a. $5.85
b. $5.99
c. $6.13
d. $6.41

33. An investor is "long 1 March corn 67 call at 3." What will the maximum gain and breakeven be on this position?

a. Unlimited gain, $70 breakeven
b. $30 gain, $70 breakeven
c. Unlimited gain, $64 breakeven
d. $3 gain, $64 breakeven

34. The number of stocks required to hedge against the price risk of holding one option is called the option's delta.

a. True
b. False

35. The purchase price of an option is the same as its strike price.

a. True
b. False

36. What is a market called where futures contracts trade at only one price?

a. Stop limit
b. Limited
c. Lock limit
d. Halted

37. Which of the following is not a difference between a futures contract and a forward contract?

a. Price is specified on a forward contract.
b. Price is set through trading on a futures contract.
c. Terms on forward contracts are standardized.
d. Terms on futures contracts are standardized.

38. What is the daily check of an investor's margin position called, that is, the gain or loss in a contract's value determined at the end of each day, when the broker debits or credits the account as needed?

a. Maintenance margin
b. Mark-to-market
c. Margin call
d. Bucketing

39. The life of a futures contract is determined by which of the following?

a. Price
b. Trading
c. Negotiation
d. Delivery month

40. Given normal market conditions, and the following table representing the wheat market at a specific point in time, which of the following would be the wheat contract price in October?

Cash Wheat	265
January	277
April	281
October	____
December	294

a. 266
b. 281
c. 286
d. 297

41. Clearinghouse member Smith Commodities establishes new long and short positions in corn futures all within the same trading day. Given their long position of 165 contracts and their short position of 45 contracts, what will be the number of contracts for which the clearinghouse will require them to deposit margin on their netted position?

a. 45 contracts
b. 120 contracts
c. 165 contracts
d. 210 contracts

42. A stop order is guaranteed to execute.

a. True
b. False

43. A crude oil contract produces a profit of 6.35 per barrel. A total of five contracts were purchased. What is the total profit made excluding commissions?

a. $3,175
b. $6,350
c. $15,875
d. $31,750

44. A market order refers to any order that is placed during market hours.

a. True
b. False

45. Which of the following is not a purpose of futures trading?

a. Safety of principal
b. Speculating
c. Spreading
d. Hedging

46. A crude oil contract produces a profit of 7.20 per barrel. With a total of four contracts purchased, profit per contract was $7,200, and the total profit on all contracts, excluding commissions, was $28,800. If a futures commission merchant charged this customer a commission of $38 per contract, what would the total net profit be, including the commission charge?

a. $7,162
b. $7,200
c. $21,638
d. $28,648

47. Which of the following interest rate yield curves is the most common?

a. Flat
b. Inverted
c. Upward sloping
d. Humped

48. What would be the total required deposit if a trader were to purchase 5 May crude oil contracts and the initial margin requirement for crude oil is $6.18 a barrel?

a. $618
b. $3,090
c. $6,180
d. $30,900

49. An investor buying 100 shares of stock and a put on the same stock at the same time is an example of a what?

a. Hedge
b. Spread
c. Straddle
d. Short

50. An investor who buys a March call on ABC at a strike price of 25 and simultaneously sells a March call at a strike price of 30 is an example of what kind of spread?

a. Bull
b. Bear
c. Vertical
d. Butterfly

51. An investor establishes the following bull call spread:

Long 1 December silver 1500 call at 6

Short 1 December silver 1700 call at 3

To what amount is this investor reducing the maximum loss to by establishing this position?

a. 3
b. 4
c. 6
d. 9

52. Established position:

Buy 4 August crude oil at 81 and Sell 4 August crude oil at 77.5

Calculate the loss (excluding commissions) per barrel, the loss per contract, and the total loss of all contracts on this position if crude oil were trading at 81 and, due to an increase in supply, dropped by 3.50.

a. $35, $35,000, $140,000
b. $3.50, $3,500, $14,000
c. $0.35, $350, $1,400
d. None of the above

53. Security futures prices are determined in their contracts rather than through continuous competitive bidding as stock prices are determined.

a. True
b. False

54. An investor buys two August corn contracts (5,000 bushels each) at 235 by depositing the initial required margin of $2,000. If the price of corn rises to 250, what is the investor's return on equity?

a. 50%
b. -75%
c. 150%
d. 75%

55. If an investor buys a silver contract (5,000 ounces per contract) at 500 and later sells at 522, what is the return on equity if the initial required margin deposited was $1,300?

a. 84.6%
b. 118.2%
c. -84.6%
d. 16.9%

56. An investor buys contract A at 433½ at the same time he or she sells contract B at 520. If he or she later sells contract A at 442 and buys contract B at 523, what is the profit and loss if dealing in cents per pound on a 5,000 pound contract?

a. $250.00
b. $275.00
c. -$550.00
d. -$275.00

57. An investor has a 3-contract position that (excluding commissions) had a per-contract loss of $2,300 and a total loss of $6,900. What would the per-contract loss and total loss be, including a commission charge of $35?

a. $2,265, $6,795
b. $1,840, $5,520
c. $2,335, $7,005
d. $2,300, $6,900

58. What is the difference between futures price and the spot price?

a. Premium
b. Basis
c. Cost
d. Delta

59. For options and futures contracts, what may interpose itself as a middleman between two traders?

a. National Futures Association (NFA)
b. Exchange
c. Clearinghouse
d. U.S. Commodity Futures Trading Commission (CFTC)

60. What is protecting the value of a portfolio with short futures positions called?

a. Long spreading
b. Short spreading
c. Long hedging
d. Short hedging

61. An increase in the money supply pushes interest rates down.

a. True
b. False

62. Interest rate levels can be affected only by the level of economic activity, changes in money supply, and Federal Reserve policies.

a. True
b. False

63. Fundamental analysis is the study of various forces at work in the workplace and their effect on stock prices.

a. True
b. False

64. A trader sells 4 October gold at 1791 AND buys 4 October gold at 1780. What is the profit per ounce, profit per contract, and total profit of all contracts (excluding commissions)?

a. $11, $110, $440
b. $44, $4,400, $17,600
c. $11, $1,100, $4,400
d. unknown, not enough information to determine

65. When will a long spot-short futures position profit?

a. When the basis narrows
b. When the basis widens
c. When the basis remains constant
d. When the basis increases

66. Given the following information, what is the option elasticity if the stock increases to $111?

Stock = $110/share

Option with $100 strike price = $5.00

Delta = 0.6

a. 12
b. 13.19
c. 0.91
d. 7.58

67. What is the rate of return that can be earned by selling a bond futures or forward contract and at the same time buying an actual bond of equal amount in the cash market using borrowed money?

a. Implied repo rate
b. Return on equity
c. Return on assets
d. Standard deviation

68. Which of the following is not used in fundamental analysis when determining a proper stock price?

a. Earnings and dividend prospects
b. Expectation of future interest rates
c. Current market conditions
d. Risk evaluation of the firm

69. Given the following long straddle, determine the breakeven point for the call and the put.

Long 1 June corn 200 Call at .47

Long 1 June corn 200 Put at .43

a. Call 290, Put 110
b. Call 200.90, Put 199.10
c. Call 290, Put 290
d. None of the above

70. What kind of signal is a price breaking through a resistance line after a particular pattern has formed in a technical analysis chart?

a. Sell
b. Hold
c. Neutral
d. Buy

71. In a technical analyst's chart, what is the price level below which a stock's price is unlikely to fall?

a. Support level
b. Resistance level
c. Trendline
d. Moving average

72. What type of an order would you place to sell a security at a specific price or better?

a. Stop
b. Limit
c. Market
d. Fill or kill

73. What would the maximum gain be on the following bull call spread?

Long 1 April wheat 38 call at 5.50

Short 1 April wheat 49 call at 2

a. 9
b. 7.50
c. 5.50
d. 11

74. What type of sell order may be placed to protect a portion of the gains on a long position?

a. Stop
b. Stop limit
c. Both A or B
d. None of the above

75. What is the most appropriate order to place to sell a long position at a specified price whenever that price is hit?

a. Stop good 'til cancelled (GTC) order
b. Stop Limit GTC order
c. Limit GTC order
d. Limit day order

76. A July 42 call, trading at $38, and with a premium of $2—given this call is "out of the money," what would its intrinsic and time value be?

a. $2 intrinsic value, $1 time value
b. no intrinsic value, $2 time value
c. $4 intrinsic value, $3 time value
d. Unknown due to lack of information to determine

77. When are option assignments normally made?

a. Within 24 to 48 hours following receipt by Options Clearing Corporation (OCC) of the exercise instruction
b. On the expiration date
c. On the same day that the OCC receives the exercise instruction
d. On the business day following receipt by OCC of the exercise instruction

78. Settlements of exercised cash-settled options are affected by clearing members and which of the following?

a. National Futures Association (NFA)
b. Options Clearing Corporation (OCC)
c. Securities & Exchange Commission (SEC)
d. Chicago Board Options Exchange (CBOE)

79. Which of the following statements regarding options transaction costs is true?

a. Transaction costs are not significant in spreads and straddles.
b. The impact of transaction costs on profitability is often greater in option transactions than in transactions in the underlying interests.
c. Transaction costs are the same regardless of whether the transactions are in effect in U.S. or foreign markets.
d. Transaction costs do not need to be discussed with an investor's brokerage firm prior to engaging in options transactions.

80. Which of the following is a risk of option holders?

a. They may be assigned an exercise at any time during the period the option is exercisable.
b. The Securities & Exchange Commission (SEC) may not impose exercise restrictions.
c. They may lose the underlying security of the option.
d. They may lose the entire amount paid for the option in a short period of time.

81. Which of the following statements is false regarding exercising options?

a. Some options are subject to automatic exercise.
b. An option holder must instruct the brokerage firm to exercise an option before the firm's cutoff.
c. An option that is not exercised by the expiration date still has value if it was in the money on the last trading day.
d. Many brokerage firms accept standing instructions to exercise an option.

82. What is the maximum potential loss for the writer of an uncovered call?

a. The amount of the premium paid
b. An unlimited amount
c. The original cost of the underlying security at the time that the option is written
d. No loss potential

83. If an investor received a premium of $5 per share for writing an uncovered ABC 55 call option and the stock price increases to $68, what is the investor's gain or loss if he or she liquidates the option position at $20 per share in an offsetting closing purchase transaction?

a. A gain of $1,500
b. A gain of $1,300
c. A loss of $1,500
d. A loss of $1,300

84. What would be the breakeven on the following bull call spread?

Long 1 June corn 41 call at 9.50

Short 1 June corn 60 call at 7

a. 38.50
b. 43.50
c. 48
d. 50.50

85. A speculator establishes a Long 1 May corn contract at 46. Due to issues with a decreased crop supply, the May delivery price increases to 52. The resulting close-out position is a sale of 1 corn contract at 52. What would be the profit on this position?

a. 4
b. 6
c. 8
d. Unknown, due not enough information

86. A registered floor broker must also register as a floor trader in order to engage in activity as a floor trader.

a. True
b. False

87. All registered introducing brokers must be members of the National Futures Association (NFA) in order to conduct futures business with the public.

a. True
b. False

88. A futures commission merchant is exempt from registration requirements if he handles transactions only for himself, his firm, or his firm's affiliates, top officers, or directors.

a. True
b. False

89. Which of the following is not a filing requirement for an associated person?

a. Fingerprint card
b. Form U-4
c. Form 8-R
d. A nonrefundable associated person application fee

90. Which of the following is not true regarding National Futures Association (NFA) membership?

a. Any person registered or provisionally registered with the commission is eligible for NFA membership.
b. Membership in NFA may be transferred or assigned.
c. Any contract market is eligible to become an NFA member.
d. There is a membership committee consisting of five directors.

91. According to National Futures Association (NFA) Compliance Rule 2-30, members must always obtain all of the following information from the customer except

a. the customer's estimated liquid net worth.
b. for individuals, the customer's approximate age or date of birth.
c. an indication of the customer's previous investment and futures trading experience.
d. the customer's true name and address.

92. Which of the following is true regarding National Futures Association (NFA) arbitration?

a. Mediation is never an option in the arbitration process.
b. The first step of the arbitration process is for the claimant to file an arbitration claim with the opposing party.
c. The first step of the arbitration process is for the claimant to file an arbitration claim with NFA.
d. The total size of the claim has no bearing on how many arbitrators there will be.

93. Can a National Futures Association (NFA) arbitration award be enforced or appealed?

a. An NFA arbitration award cannot be enforced, but it can be appealed.
b. An NFA arbitration award can be enforced, but it cannot be appealed.
c. An NFA arbitration award cannot be enforced or appealed.
d. An NFA arbitration award can be enforced and appealed.

94. An arbitration claim must be filed within what time period from the date that a customer knew, or should have known, of the acts or transactions that form the basis for the claim?

a. 12 months
b. 18 months
c. 2 years
d. 3 years

95. What is the premium on an October Treasury bond futures 97 call that is being quoted at 1.24?

a. $12.40
b. $1,037.50
c. $1,240
d. $1,375

96. What is the minimum experience required for an associated person to exercise discretion over a customer's commodity futures account?

a. The associate must be continuously registered for 1 year and have worked in such registered capacity for that period of time.
b. The associate must be continuously registered for 2 years and have worked in such registered capacity for that period of time.
c. The associate must be continuously registered for 3 years and have worked in such registered capacity for that period of time.
d. The associate must be continuously registered for 5 years and have worked in such registered capacity for that period of time.

97. Which of the following would be considered an "in the money" option?

a. February gold 99 call, February gold is trading at 109
b. March wheat 80 call, March wheat is trading at 68
c. August silver 136 call, July silver is trading at 151
d. November corn 56 call, November corn is trading at 56

98. The commodity pool operator (CPO) of a commodity pool that is required to register its securities under the Securities Act of 1933 must deliver what document in addition to the disclosure document prior to accepting or receiving funds from a prospective participant?

a. Prospectus
b. Annual report
c. Financial statements
d. Statement of additional information

99. According to the National Futures Association (NFA) Compliance Rule 2-29, promotional material may not include statements of opinion.

a. True
b. False

100. Which of the following is not defined as *promotional material* by the National Futures Association (NFA) Compliance Rule 2-29?

a. Newspaper ad
b. Standardized report, which is directed to the public
c. text of a radio ad
d. mutual fund prospectus

101. What is the premium on a Treasury bill futures option that is being quoted at 3.5 percent?

a. $3,500
b. $8,750
c. $350
d. $875

102. The cover page of the disclosure document for commodity trading advisors (CTAs) must display the cautionary statement in capital letters and boldface type.

a. True
b. False

103. The disclosure document's description of the trading program must always include all of the following except

a. the types of commodity interest that the commodity trading advisor (CTA) intends to trade.
b. any restrictions or limitation on trading established by the trading advisor.
c. the types of other interest that the CTA intends to trade.
d. the method for how futures commission merchants (FCMs) or RFEDs carrying accounts it manages treat offsetting positions.

104. The commodity trading advisor's (CTA's) disclosure document must include a description of each fee the CTA will charge. How must these fees be specified whenever possible?

a. In dollar amounts
b. In percentages
c. Average dollar amount
d. A range of the highest and lowest fees that may be charged

105. The commodity trading advisor's (CTA's) disclosure document must include only actual conflicts of interest.

a. True
b. False

106. If a member futures commission merchant's (FCM's) adjusted net capital falls below the early warning requirement or eligibility to guarantee an introducing broker's (IB's) requirement, notification is required within what time frame?

a. 12 hours
b. 24 hours
c. 36 hours
d. 48 hours

107. How often must a futures commission merchant (FCM) submit unaudited financial reports?

a. Quarterly, within 17 business days of quarter end
b. Quarterly, within 19 business days of quarter end
c. Monthly, within 17 business days of month end
d. Monthly, within 19 business days of month end

108. How often must futures commission merchants (FCMs) file position reports with the U.S. Commodity Futures Trading Commission?

a. Daily
b. Weekly
c. Biweekly
d. Monthly

109. Guaranteed introducing brokers (IBs) that have filed the appropriate guarantee agreement are not subject to the minimum net capital or financial reporting requirements.

a. True
b. False

110. Calculate the beta-adjusted value at risk of a portfolio if the portfolio's value is $60 million with a portfolio beta of 1.65.

a. $36,364,000
b. $99,000
c. $99,000,000
d. $990

111. Passed in 1936, which of the following regulates the trading of commodity futures in the United States?

a. Dodd–Frank Act
b. The Securities Act of 1933
c. The Commodity Exchange Act
d. Sarbanes–Oxley Act

112. Which of the following is true regarding a member responsibility action (MRA)?

a. An MRA is issued by the Securities & Exchange Commission (SEC).
b. An MRA is an award given by the National Futures Association (NFA).
c. An MRA can promote a member or associate.
d. An MRA can suspend a member or associate.

113. If a member has been issued a member responsibility action (MRA), challenges it, and has a hearing but does not agree with the outcome, the member may not appeal the decision.

a. True
b. False

114. An answer to the complaint must be filed within how many days of the National Futures Association's (NFA's) Business Conduct Committee issuing the complaint?

a. 30
b. 45
c. 60
d. 75

115. What is the time limit for an investor to file an arbitration claim at the National Futures Association (NFA)?

a. 1 year
b. 2 years
c. 5 years
d. None

116. Which of the following statements is false regarding award, settlement, and withdrawal in member arbitration?

a. The award may grant or deny any of the relief requested.
b. The panel's award shall be final.
c. There is a right to appeal the award.
d. At any time during the arbitration, the parties may agree to satisfy a claim.

117. In an arbitration hearing, the panel must apply the technical rules of evidence.

a. True
b. False

118. The owner of a wheat farm made a best-guess prediction for his next crop at 106,500 bushels. If trying to hedge utilizing futures contracts that cover 5,000 bushels of wheat, how many contracts should he sell to hedge his entire crop?

a. 21.3
b. 21
c. 22
d. None of the above

119. What are acceptable margin deposits and their collateral values dictated by?

a. The introducing broker (IB)
b. The futures commission merchant (FCM)
c. Each firm
d. Individual exchanges

120. Who is responsible for making a bona fide attempt to collect funds to satisfy a margin call?

a. Futures commission merchant (FCM)
b. Introducing broker (IB)
c. Chief technical officer (CTO)
d. Commodity trading Advisor (CTA)

Answer Key and Explanations

1. C: Churning is excessive trading that results in increased commissions for the broker while providing no benefit to the customer.

2. B: The tendency for prices of physical commodities and futures to approach one another, usually during the delivery month, is convergence.

3. A: An associated person is an individual who solicits orders, customers, or customer funds on behalf of a futures commission merchant, an introducing broker, a commodity trading advisor, or a commodity pool operator and is registered with the Commodity Futures Trading Commission.

4. C: A floor broker is an individual who executes orders on the trading floor of an exchange for any other person.

5. D: A scalper is a trader who trades for small, short-term profits during one trading session and rarely holds a position overnight.

6. D: A tick is the smallest increment of a price movement for a futures contract.

7. A: An option writer can also be referred to as an option seller.

8. B: The premium is the price that the holder of an option pays and the writer of an option receives for the rights conveyed by the option. The strike price is another name for the exercise price.

9. A: A call option is in the money if the current market value of the underlying security is above the exercise price of the option.

10. A: Intrinsic value is the amount, if any, that an option is in the money.

11. B: If the exercise price of a put is below the current market value of the underlying security, it is considered to be out of the money.

12. B: When computing margin calls, option values of all options contracts are allowed to meet an account's total risk margin requirement.

13. C: A performance bond is also referred to as margin.

14. B: A futures contract does not specify a strike price. It specifies the item being bought and sold, the contract month, the manner of settlement, and the standardized contract size.

15. A: A feature of futures trading whose risks are the mirror image of its potential benefits is leverage.

16. D: Establishing a position in the futures market that is equal and opposite to a position in the cash market is called hedging.

17. B: Gains and losses are credited or debited to the accounts of buyers and sellers of futures contracts daily.

18. A: The minimum margin requirement for security futures set by law is 20% of the contract value.

19. C: The initial margin requirement on the purchase of a futures contract worth $5,000 is $1,000 (20%).

20. D: A spread is when an investor takes a long position in a futures contract of one maturity and a short position in a contract on the same commodity with a different maturity.

21. D: An investor having purchased 5 September wheat futures contracts at 7.35 would like to protect and maximize the profit given his desire to sell sometime in the near future. The contracts are trading at a high of 9.85, but the investor believes that the price will begin to drop, possibly to as low as 7.50. The order he should enter to protect and maximize those profits is "sell 5 September wheat futures at 9.25 stop." If these contracts trade down to or through 9.25, a market order will be triggered to sell at that price, thus providing a profit for that investor. A "sell 5 September wheat futures at 8.25 stop" order will provide profit but less than the order to sell at 9.25. A "sell 5 September wheat futures at 7.25 stop" will NOT provide any profit given the 7.25 sell price is below the purchase price of 7.35.

22. D: An investor who purchased 17 April corn futures contracts at 14.50 would maximize profits here by selling at 15.75. Selling at 15.25 would provide some profit but less than 15.75, and selling at either 14.00 or 14.25 would produce a loss, having purchased the contracts at 14.50.

23. B: In the futures industry, margin is a deposit of funds with the brokerage firm to provide a reserve to cover potential losses. When purchasing stocks, margin refers to a partial payment for the stock being purchased.

24. B: Buyers of futures contracts have no ownership interests or voting rights and receive no dividends.

25. A: Failure to meet a margin call within the time period allowed may result in the broker liquidating a customer's open futures positions at the current market price without prior notice.

26. C: Purchasing 9 May silver futures contracts at 55.75 will allow this investor to cover the short position while additionally making a profit from buying at 55.75 and selling at 57.25. Purchasing at 57.00 is still below the sale price but barely and still less (if any) potential profit than the 55.75 option. Both 57.75 and 58.25 are purchase prices that are higher than this investor's sale price, thus profit potential would be eliminated here.

27. A: The request for additional margin is a margin call.

28. B: The amount of the margin call is $2,000. Because the amount of funds fell below the maintenance requirement, deposit enough funds must be deposited to restore the account to the initial requirement of $5,000.

29. D: Futures contracts began trading in the United States in 1865.

30. D: If a Standard & Poor's (S&P) 500 index futures contract is currently trading at a price of 145-00, the intrinsic value of a call option conveying the right to purchase that futures contract at a strike price of 135-00 is $1,000. S&P 500 index options conventionally have a 100x contract multiplier, in which case a $10 difference between the currently traded price and the strike price ($145 - $135) would yield a $1,000 intrinsic value.

31. C: The maximum gain on this position is simply the premium the investor was paid when he sold the call.

$$3 \times \$100 = \$300$$

The maximum loss on this position is unlimited. The investor in selling this call is hoping that the price of the underlying futures contract will decrease. In the event that it increases, the buyer of the call will want to exercise his option at the contracted lower price. Having sold this call short and without ownership of the underlying futures contract, the investor will then have to purchase the contract at the now-increased price to cover the call. Because the potential price increase of the contract is without limits, so too this investor's potential loss is also without limits.

$$\begin{aligned} \text{Breakeven} &= \text{Strike Price} + \text{Premium} \\ \$603 &= 600 + 3 \end{aligned}$$

32. D:

$$\begin{aligned} (\$0.11 + \$0.03) &= \$0.14 \text{ total carrying cost for corn per bushel per month} \\ (\$0.14 \times 4) &= \$0.56 \text{ total carrying cost for corn per bushel over 4 months} \\ (\$5.85 + \$0.56) &= \$6.41 \text{ total cost per bushel to buy the corn and hold onto it for 4 months} \end{aligned}$$

33. A: The investor's maximum gain on this position is unlimited in that profit on this position comes from an increase in the futures contract price. There is no limit on how high the price may increase, and accordingly, the potential gain has no limit also.

$$\begin{aligned} \text{Breakeven} &= \text{Strike Price} + \text{Premium} \\ \$70 &= 67 + 3 \end{aligned}$$

34. A: The number of stocks required to hedge against the price risk of holding one option is called the option's delta.

35. B: The purchase of price of an option is the same as its premium.

36. C: A lock limit market is when futures contracts are traded only at the exchange's predetermined price. Price fluctuations are disallowed to prevent investors from incurring significant losses.

37. C: Terms on forward contracts are not standardized.

38. B: The daily check of an investor's margin position, the gain or loss in a contract's value determined at the end of each day, when the broker debits or credits the account as needed, is called mark-to-market.

39. D: The life of a futures contract is determined by the delivery month.

40. C: Given normal market conditions, and the information provided in the table, the wheat contract price in October would be 286. Normal market conditions dictate that contract prices be trading above the price of the cash commodity. Further, all successive prices must increase the farther out in delivery month you go. Here the price of cash wheat is 265. The 286 price is the only choice that is both higher than the cash wheat price of 265, and above the April price of 281, but below the December price of 294.

41. B: Clearinghouse member Smith Commodities establishes new long and short positions in corn futures all within the same trading day. Given the long position of 165 contracts and the short position of 45 contracts, the clearinghouse will require Smith to deposit margin on 120 contracts. The clearinghouse will be calculating the amount of margin required for deposit based on Smith's netted position.

$$165 \text{ long contracts} - 45 \text{ short contracts} = 120 \text{ contracts}$$

42. B: A stop order is not guaranteed to execute. If the market price is moving too rapidly, there may be no time to liquidate the position.

43. D: Each oil contract represents 1,000 barrels of oil.

$$\text{Profit per contract} = \text{profit per barrel} \times 1{,}000 \text{ barrels}$$
$$\text{Profit per contract} = 6.35 \times 1{,}000 = \$6{,}350$$

$$\text{Total profit on all contracts} = \text{profit per contract} \times \text{\# of contracts}$$
$$\text{Total profit on all contracts} = \$6{,}350 \times 5 = \$31{,}750$$

44. B: A market order is an order to buy or sell at the best available price when the order is placed.

45. A: Safety of principal is not a purpose of futures trading. Futures trading involves risk and is not suitable for all investors.

46. D:

$$\text{Total net profit per contract} = \text{total profit per contract} - \text{commission per contract}$$
$$\text{Total net profit per contract} = \$7{,}200 - \$38 = \$7{,}162$$

$$\text{Total net profit on all contracts} = \text{total profit per contract} \times \text{\# of contracts}$$
$$\text{Total net profit on all contracts} = \$7{,}162 \times 4 = \$28{,}648$$

47. C: The most common interest rate yield curve is upward sloping. It shows that yields increase with longer maturities.

48. D: Each crude oil contract represents 1,000 barrels of oil.

$$\text{Initial margin requirement per contract} = \text{initial margin requirement} \times 1{,}000 \text{ barrels}$$
$$\text{Initial margin requirement per contract} = 6.18 \times 1{,}000 = \$6{,}180$$

$$\text{Total required deposit} = \text{initial margin requirement per contract} \times \text{\# of contracts}$$
$$\text{Total required deposit} = \$6{,}180 \times 5 = \$30{,}900$$

49. A: An investor buying 100 shares of stock and a put on the same stock at the same time is an example of a hedge. This type of hedge is a protective put.

50. C: An investor who buys a March call on ABC at a strike price of 25 and simultaneously sells a March call at a strike price of 30 is an example of a vertical spread.

51. A: If this investor had only purchased the 1 December silver 1500 call at 6, the maximum loss would have been 6.

$$6 - 3 = 3$$

By also selling the 1 December silver 1700 call at 3, he has reduced the maximum loss from 6 to 3.

52. B:

$$81.0 - 77.5 = 3.5 \text{ loss per barrel}$$

Given that each crude oil contract represents 1,000 barrels of oil:

$$\text{Loss per contract} = \text{loss per barrel} \times 1{,}000 \text{ barrels}$$
$$\text{Loss per contract} = \$3.50 \times 1{,}000 = \$3{,}500$$

$$\text{Loss of all contracts} = \text{loss per contract} \times \# \text{ of contracts}$$
$$\text{Loss of all contracts} = \$3{,}500 \times 4 = \$14{,}000$$

53. B: Security futures prices are determined through continuous competitive bidding just as stock prices are determined.

54. D: An investor buys two August corn contracts (5,000 bushels each) @ 235 by depositing the initial required margin of $2,000. If the price of corn rises to 250, the investor's return on equity is 75% (1500/2000).

55. A: If an investor buys a silver contract (5,000 ounces per contract) at 500 and later sells at 522, the return on equity, if the initial required margin deposited was $1,300, is 84.6% (1100/1300).

56. B: An investor buys contract A at 433½; at the same time, he sells contract B at 520. If he or she later sells contract A at 442 and buys contract B at 523, the profit, if dealing in cents per pound on a 5,000 pound contract, is $275.00 (0.055*5000).

57. C:

$$\text{Loss per contract} = \text{per contract loss} + \text{commission charge}$$
$$\text{Loss per contract} = \$2{,}300 + \$35 = \$2{,}335$$

$$\text{Total net loss} = \text{loss per contract} \times \# \text{ of contracts}$$
$$\text{Total net loss} = \$2{,}335 \times 3 = \$7{,}005$$

58. B: Basis is the difference between the futures price and the spot price.

59. C: For options and futures contracts, the clearinghouse may interpose itself as a middleman between two traders.

60. D: Protecting the value of a portfolio with short futures positions is called short hedging.

61. A: An increase in the money supply pushes interest rates down.

62. B: Interest rate levels can be affected by many factors besides the level of economic activity, changes in money supply, and Federal Reserve policies. Other factors include the size of the federal budget deficit and interest rate levels in foreign markets.

63. B: Fundamental analysis is the study of the financial condition and operation results of a firm. Technical analysis is the study of various forces at work in the workplace and their effect on stock prices.

64. C:

$$\text{Profit per ounce } = 1{,}791 - 1{,}780 \ = \$11 \text{ per troy ounce}$$

Each gold contract represents 100 troy ounces.

$$\text{Profit per contract } = \text{profit per ounce } \times 100 \text{ ounces}$$
$$\text{Profit per contract } = \$11 \ \times 100 \ = \$1{,}100$$

$$\text{Total profit of all contracts } = \text{profit per contract } \times \# \text{ of contracts}$$
$$\text{Total profit of all contracts } = \$1{,}100 \ \times 4 \ = \$4{,}400$$

65. A: A long spot-short futures position will profit when the basis narrows.

66. B: The option elasticity is 13.19 (12/.91).

67. A: The rate of return that can be earned by selling a bond futures or forward contract while at the same time buying an actual bond of equal amount in the cash market using borrowed money is the implied repo rate.

68. C: The current market conditions are not used in fundamental analysis when determining a proper stock price.

69. A:

$$\text{Total premium } = \text{call premium} + \text{put premium}$$
$$\text{Total premium } = \ (.47 \ \times 100) + \ (.43 \ \times 100)$$
$$= 47 + 43 \ = 90$$

$$\text{Breakeven for call side } = \text{call strike price} + \text{total premium}$$
$$\text{Breakeven for call side } = 200 + 90 \ = 290$$

$$\text{Breakeven for put side } = \text{put strike price} - \text{total premium}$$
$$\text{Breakeven for put side } = 200 - 90 \ = 110$$

70. D: A price breaking through a resistance line after a particular pattern has formed in a technical analysis chart is a buy signal.

71. A: In a technical analyst's chart, the price levels below which a stock's price is unlikely to fall is the support level.

72. B: An order that you would place to sell a security at a specific price or better is a limit order.

73. B:

$$\text{Maximum gain on bull call spread } = \text{difference in strike prices} - \text{net premium paid}$$
$$\text{Maximum gain on bull call spread } = \ (49 - 38) - \ (5.50 - 2)$$
$$= 11 - 3.50 \ = 7.50$$

The maximum gain will be realized by this investor if both options are exercised.

74. C: Both a stop and a stop limit sell order may be placed to protect a portion of the gains on a long position.

75. C: A limit good-'til-canceled (GTC) order is the most appropriate order to place if you want to sell a long position at a specified price whenever that price is hit.

76. B: A July 42 call, trading at $38, and with a premium of $2, is "out of the money." Given an option's intrinsic value is the amount the option is "in the money," this option would have no intrinsic value. The time value of this option equals its premium value above its intrinsic value and is the price that is paid for the "option" or opportunity to buy or sell at the contracted price. With that, its time value would be the option's entire premium value of $2 because the option has no intrinsic value.

77. D: Option assignments are normally made the business day following receipt by Options Clearing Corporation (OCC) of the exercise instruction.

78. B: Settlements of exercised cash-settled options are affected by clearing members and the Options Clearing Corporation (OCC).

79. B: The impact of transaction costs on profitability is often greater in option transactions than in transactions in the underlying interests.

80. D: An option holder may lose the entire amount paid for the option in a short period of time. Being assigned an exercise at any time during the period the option is exercisable and losing the underlying security are risks of an option writer. It is not a risk if the Security & Exchange Commission (SEC) may not impose exercise restrictions. The risk is that the SEC or another regulatory agency may impose exercise restrictions.

81. C: An option that is not exercised by the expiration date is worthless.

82. B: The maximum potential loss for the writer of an uncovered call is unlimited. Because the uncovered call writer does not own the underlying security, he or she must purchase that security at the current market price when the option is exercised. As there is no limit as to how high the underlying security's price may increase, the cost to an uncovered call writer is unlimited.

83. C: If an investor received a premium of $5 per share for writing an uncovered ABC 55 call option and the stock price increases to $68, the investor's loss, if he or she liquidates the option position at $20 per share in an offsetting closing purchase transaction, is $1,500 ($2,000 paid in the offsetting transaction less the $500 option premium received when the option was written).

84. B:

$$\begin{aligned}\text{Breakeven on bull call spread} &= \text{lower strike price} + \text{net premium}\\ \text{Breakeven on bull call spread} &= 41 + (9.50 - 7)\\ &= 41 + 2.50 = 43.50\end{aligned}$$

85. B:

Purchased 1 May corn contract at 46

Sold 1 May corn contract at 52

$$\text{Profit} = 52 - 46 = 6$$

86. B: A registered floor broker does not need to register also as a floor trader in order to engage in activity as a floor trader.

87. A: All registered introducing brokers must be members of the National Futures Association (NFA) to conduct futures business with the public.

88. A: A futures commission merchant is exempt from registration requirements if he handles transactions only for himself, his firm, or his firm's affiliates, top officers, or directors.

89. B: A Form U-4 is not a filing requirement for an associated person.

90. B: National Futures Association (NFA) membership may not be transferred or assigned.

91. A: According to National Futures Association (NFA) Compliance Rule 2-30, the customer's estimated liquid net worth needs to be obtained by a member only when the member is not also a member of the Financial Industry Regulatory Authority.

92. C: The first step of the arbitration process is for the claimant to file an arbitration claim with the National Futures Association (NFA). Mediation is available as part of the arbitration process, and the total size of the claim dictates how many arbitrators there will be (one or three).

93. B: A National Futures Association (NFA) arbitration award can be enforced, but it cannot be appealed.

94. C: An arbitration claim must be filed within two years from the date that a customer knew, or should have known, of the acts or transactions that form the basis for the claim.

95. D:

$$\begin{aligned} 1.24 &= 1\frac{24}{64}\% \times \$100{,}000 \\ 1.375\% \times \$100{,}000 &= \$1{,}375 \end{aligned}$$

96. B: The minimum experience required for an associated person to exercise discretion over a customer's commodity futures account is that the associate must be continuously registered for two years and have worked in such a registered capacity for that period of time.

97. A: An "in the money" call option has a futures contract price that is greater than the option strike price. Here the February gold 99 call (when February gold is trading at 109) is the "in the money" option. The owner of this call option could exercise the option to buy the underlying futures contract at 99 and then potentially sell it at its current price of 109 for a profit. The March wheat 80 call is "out of the money" (when March wheat is trading at 68) because the call option has a futures contract price that is lower than the option strike price. The November corn 56 call is "at the money" (when November corn is trading at 56) because the call option has a futures contract price that is equal to the option strike price. It is unknown whether the August silver 136 call is "in the money" due to the August silver trading price not being provided.

98. D: The commodity pool operator (CPO) of a commodity pool that is required to register its securities under the Securities Act of 1933 must deliver a statement of additional information in addition to the disclosure document prior to accepting or receiving funds from a prospective participant.

99. B: According to a National Futures Association (NFA) Compliance Rule 2-29, promotional material may include statements of opinion as long as they are clearly identifiable as such and have a reasonable basis in fact.

100. D: A mutual fund prospectus is not included in the definition of *promotional material* in National Futures Association (NFA) Compliance Rule 2-29. In this rule, "promotional material includes: (i) Any text of a standardized oral presentation, or any communication for publication in any newspaper, magazine or similar medium, or for broadcast over television, radio, or other electronic medium, which is disseminated or directed to the public concerning a futures account, agreement or transaction; (ii) any standardized form of report, letter, circular, memorandum or publication which is disseminated or directed to the public; and (iii) any other written material disseminated or directed to the public for the purpose of soliciting a futures account, agreement or transaction."

101. B:

$$3.5\% \times \$1{,}000{,}000 = \$35{,}000$$
$$\frac{\$35{,}000}{4} = \$8{,}750$$

102. A: The cover page of the disclosure document for commodity training advisors (CTAs) must include prominently the cautionary statement. *Prominently* means displayed in capital letters and in boldface type.

103. D: The disclosure document's description of the trading program must always include all of the following except the method for how futures commission merchants (FCMs) or RFEDs carrying accounts the manages treat offsetting positions. The method only needs to be disclosed if they are not on a first-in, first-out basis or to close out all offsetting positions.

104. A: The commodity training advisor's (CTA's) disclosure document must include a description of each fee that the CTA will charge. The document must specify the dollar amount of each fee whenever possible.

105. B: The commodity training advisor's (CTA's) disclosure document must include actual and potential conflicts of interest.

106. B: If a member futures commission merchant's (FCM's) adjusted net capital falls below the early warning requirement or eligibility to guarantee the introducing broker's (IB's) requirement, notification is required within 24 hours.

107. C: A futures commission merchant (FCM) must submit unaudited financial reports monthly within 17 business days of month end.

108. A: Futures commission merchants (FCMs) file position reports with the U.S. Commodity Futures Trading Commission daily.

109. A: Guaranteed introducing brokers (IBs) that have filed the appropriate guarantee agreement are not subject to the minimum net capital or financial reporting requirements.

110. C:

$$\$60{,}000{,}000 \times 1.65 = \$99{,}000{,}000$$

111. C: The Commodity Exchange Act, passed in 1936, regulates the trading of commodity futures in the United States.

112. D: A member responsibility action (MRA) is issued by the National Futures Association (NFA. It can suspend the Member or Associate, order the Member or Associate to restrict its operations, or direct the Member or Associate to take other remedial action.

113. B: If a member has been issued a member responsibility action (MRA), challenges it, and has a hearing but does not agree with the outcome, the member may appeal the decision to the U.S. Commodity Futures Trading Commission (CFTC).

114. A: An answer to the complaint must be filed within 30 days of the National Futures Association's (NFA's) Business Conduct Committee issuing the complaint.

115. B: The time limit for an investor to file an arbitration claim at the National Futures Association (NFA) is two years.

116. C: In member arbitration, there is no right of appeal of the award.

117. B: In an arbitration hearing, the panel does not need to apply the technical rules of evidence.

118. C:

$$\frac{106{,}500}{5{,}000} = 21.3$$

It's not possible for this farmer to sell 21.3 contracts. The question then becomes what the appropriate number to sell is to best hedge the entire crop. He should sell 22 contracts. It's not a good choice to over-hedge this position with a higher number of contracts and end up speculating on additional bushels as a result.

119. D: Acceptable margin deposits and their collateral value are dictated by the individual exchanges.

120. A: The futures commission merchant (FCM) is responsible for making a bona-fide attempt to collect funds to satisfy a margin call.

How to Overcome Test Anxiety

Just the thought of taking a test is enough to make most people a little nervous. A test is an important event that can have a long-term impact on your future, so it's important to take it seriously and it's natural to feel anxious about performing well. But just because anxiety is normal, that doesn't mean that it's helpful in test taking, or that you should simply accept it as part of your life. Anxiety can have a variety of effects. These effects can be mild, like making you feel slightly nervous, or severe, like blocking your ability to focus or remember even a simple detail.

If you experience test anxiety—whether severe or mild—it's important to know how to beat it. To discover this, first you need to understand what causes test anxiety.

Causes of Test Anxiety

While we often think of anxiety as an uncontrollable emotional state, it can actually be caused by simple, practical things. One of the most common causes of test anxiety is that a person does not feel adequately prepared for their test. This feeling can be the result of many different issues such as poor study habits or lack of organization, but the most common culprit is time management. Starting to study too late, failing to organize your study time to cover all of the material, or being distracted while you study will mean that you're not well prepared for the test. This may lead to cramming the night before, which will cause you to be physically and mentally exhausted for the test. Poor time management also contributes to feelings of stress, fear, and hopelessness as you realize you are not well prepared but don't know what to do about it.

Other times, test anxiety is not related to your preparation for the test but comes from unresolved fear. This may be a past failure on a test, or poor performance on tests in general. It may come from comparing yourself to others who seem to be performing better or from the stress of living up to expectations. Anxiety may be driven by fears of the future—how failure on this test would affect your educational and career goals. These fears are often completely irrational, but they can still negatively impact your test performance.

Review Video: 3 Reasons You Have Test Anxiety
Visit mometrix.com/academy and enter code: 428468

Elements of Test Anxiety

As mentioned earlier, test anxiety is considered to be an emotional state, but it has physical and mental components as well. Sometimes you may not even realize that you are suffering from test anxiety until you notice the physical symptoms. These can include trembling hands, rapid heartbeat, sweating, nausea, and tense muscles. Extreme anxiety may lead to fainting or vomiting. Obviously, any of these symptoms can have a negative impact on testing. It is important to recognize them as soon as they begin to occur so that you can address the problem before it damages your performance.

Review Video: 3 Ways to Tell You Have Test Anxiety
Visit mometrix.com/academy and enter code: 927847

The mental components of test anxiety include trouble focusing and inability to remember learned information. During a test, your mind is on high alert, which can help you recall information and stay focused for an extended period of time. However, anxiety interferes with your mind's natural processes, causing you to blank out, even on the questions you know well. The strain of testing during anxiety makes it difficult to stay focused, especially on a test that may take several hours. Extreme anxiety can take a huge mental toll, making it difficult not only to recall test information but even to understand the test questions or pull your thoughts together.

Review Video: How Test Anxiety Affects Memory
Visit mometrix.com/academy and enter code: 609003

Effects of Test Anxiety

Test anxiety is like a disease—if left untreated, it will get progressively worse. Anxiety leads to poor performance, and this reinforces the feelings of fear and failure, which in turn lead to poor performances on subsequent tests. It can grow from a mild nervousness to a crippling condition. If allowed to progress, test anxiety can have a big impact on your schooling, and consequently on your future.

Test anxiety can spread to other parts of your life. Anxiety on tests can become anxiety in any stressful situation, and blanking on a test can turn into panicking in a job situation. But fortunately, you don't have to let anxiety rule your testing and determine your grades. There are a number of relatively simple steps you can take to move past anxiety and function normally on a test and in the rest of life.

Review Video: How Test Anxiety Impacts Your Grades
Visit mometrix.com/academy and enter code: 939819

Physical Steps for Beating Test Anxiety

While test anxiety is a serious problem, the good news is that it can be overcome. It doesn't have to control your ability to think and remember information. While it may take time, you can begin taking steps today to beat anxiety.

Just as your first hint that you may be struggling with anxiety comes from the physical symptoms, the first step to treating it is also physical. Rest is crucial for having a clear, strong mind. If you are tired, it is much easier to give in to anxiety. But if you establish good sleep habits, your body and mind will be ready to perform optimally, without the strain of exhaustion. Additionally, sleeping well helps you to retain information better, so you're more likely to recall the answers when you see the test questions.

Getting good sleep means more than going to bed on time. It's important to allow your brain time to relax. Take study breaks from time to time so it doesn't get overworked, and don't study right before bed. Take time to rest your mind before trying to rest your body, or you may find it difficult to fall asleep.

Review Video: The Importance of Sleep for Your Brain
Visit mometrix.com/academy and enter code: 319338

Along with sleep, other aspects of physical health are important in preparing for a test. Good nutrition is vital for good brain function. Sugary foods and drinks may give a burst of energy but this burst is followed by a crash, both physically and emotionally. Instead, fuel your body with protein and vitamin-rich foods.

Also, drink plenty of water. Dehydration can lead to headaches and exhaustion, especially if your brain is already under stress from the rigors of the test. Particularly if your test is a long one, drink water during the breaks. And if possible, take an energy-boosting snack to eat between sections.

Review Video: How Diet Can Affect your Mood
Visit mometrix.com/academy and enter code: 624317

Along with sleep and diet, a third important part of physical health is exercise. Maintaining a steady workout schedule is helpful, but even taking 5-minute study breaks to walk can help get your blood pumping faster and clear your head. Exercise also releases endorphins, which contribute to a positive feeling and can help combat test anxiety.

When you nurture your physical health, you are also contributing to your mental health. If your body is healthy, your mind is much more likely to be healthy as well. So take time to rest, nourish your body with healthy food and water, and get moving as much as possible. Taking these physical steps will make you stronger and more able to take the mental steps necessary to overcome test anxiety.

Review Video: How to Stay Healthy and Prevent Test Anxiety
Visit mometrix.com/academy and enter code: 877894

Mental Steps for Beating Test Anxiety

Working on the mental side of test anxiety can be more challenging, but as with the physical side, there are clear steps you can take to overcome it. As mentioned earlier, test anxiety often stems from lack of preparation, so the obvious solution is to prepare for the test. Effective studying may be the most important weapon you have for beating test anxiety, but you can and should employ several other mental tools to combat fear.

First, boost your confidence by reminding yourself of past success—tests or projects that you aced. If you're putting as much effort into preparing for this test as you did for those, there's no reason you should expect to fail here. Work hard to prepare; then trust your preparation.

Second, surround yourself with encouraging people. It can be helpful to find a study group, but be sure that the people you're around will encourage a positive attitude. If you spend time with others who are anxious or cynical, this will only contribute to your own anxiety. Look for others who are motivated to study hard from a desire to succeed, not from a fear of failure.

Third, reward yourself. A test is physically and mentally tiring, even without anxiety, and it can be helpful to have something to look forward to. Plan an activity following the test, regardless of the outcome, such as going to a movie or getting ice cream.

When you are taking the test, if you find yourself beginning to feel anxious, remind yourself that you know the material. Visualize successfully completing the test. Then take a few deep, relaxing breaths and return to it. Work through the questions carefully but with confidence, knowing that you are capable of succeeding.

Developing a healthy mental approach to test taking will also aid in other areas of life. Test anxiety affects more than just the actual test—it can be damaging to your mental health and even contribute to depression. It's important to beat test anxiety before it becomes a problem for more than testing.

Review Video: Test Anxiety and Depression
Visit mometrix.com/academy and enter code: 904704

Study Strategy

Being prepared for the test is necessary to combat anxiety, but what does being prepared look like? You may study for hours on end and still not feel prepared. What you need is a strategy for test prep. The next few pages outline our recommended steps to help you plan out and conquer the challenge of preparation.

Step 1: Scope Out the Test

Learn everything you can about the format (multiple choice, essay, etc.) and what will be on the test. Gather any study materials, course outlines, or sample exams that may be available. Not only will this help you to prepare, but knowing what to expect can help to alleviate test anxiety.

Step 2: Map Out the Material

Look through the textbook or study guide and make note of how many chapters or sections it has. Then divide these over the time you have. For example, if a book has 15 chapters and you have five days to study, you need to cover three chapters each day. Even better, if you have the time, leave an extra day at the end for overall review after you have gone through the material in depth.

If time is limited, you may need to prioritize the material. Look through it and make note of which sections you think you already have a good grasp on, and which need review. While you are studying, skim quickly through the familiar sections and take more time on the challenging parts. Write out your plan so you don't get lost as you go. Having a written plan also helps you feel more in control of the study, so anxiety is less likely to arise from feeling overwhelmed at the amount to cover.

Step 3: Gather Your Tools

Decide what study method works best for you. Do you prefer to highlight in the book as you study and then go back over the highlighted portions? Or do you type out notes of the important information? Or is it helpful to make flashcards that you can carry with you? Assemble the pens, index cards, highlighters, post-it notes, and any other materials you may need so you won't be distracted by getting up to find things while you study.

If you're having a hard time retaining the information or organizing your notes, experiment with different methods. For example, try color-coding by subject with colored pens, highlighters, or post-it notes. If you learn better by hearing, try recording yourself reading your notes so you can listen while in the car, working out, or simply sitting at your desk. Ask a friend to quiz you from your flashcards, or try teaching someone the material to solidify it in your mind.

Step 4: Create Your Environment

It's important to avoid distractions while you study. This includes both the obvious distractions like visitors and the subtle distractions like an uncomfortable chair (or a too-comfortable couch that makes you want to fall asleep). Set up the best study environment possible: good lighting and a comfortable work area. If background music helps you focus, you may want to turn it on, but otherwise keep the room quiet. If you are using a computer to take notes, be sure you don't have any other windows open, especially applications like social media, games, or anything else that could distract you. Silence your phone and turn off notifications. Be sure to keep water close by so you stay hydrated while you study (but avoid unhealthy drinks and snacks).

Also, take into account the best time of day to study. Are you freshest first thing in the morning? Try to set aside some time then to work through the material. Is your mind clearer in the afternoon or evening? Schedule your study session then. Another method is to study at the same time of day that you will take the test, so that your brain gets used to working on the material at that time and will be ready to focus at test time.

Step 5: Study!

Once you have done all the study preparation, it's time to settle into the actual studying. Sit down, take a few moments to settle your mind so you can focus, and begin to follow your study plan. Don't give in to distractions or let yourself procrastinate. This is your time to prepare so you'll be ready to fearlessly approach the test. Make the most of the time and stay focused.

Of course, you don't want to burn out. If you study too long you may find that you're not retaining the information very well. Take regular study breaks. For example, taking five minutes out of every hour to walk briskly, breathing deeply and swinging your arms, can help your mind stay fresh.

As you get to the end of each chapter or section, it's a good idea to do a quick review. Remind yourself of what you learned and work on any difficult parts. When you feel that you've mastered the material, move on to the next part. At the end of your study session, briefly skim through your notes again.

But while review is helpful, cramming last minute is NOT. If at all possible, work ahead so that you won't need to fit all your study into the last day. Cramming overloads your brain with more information than it can process and retain, and your tired mind may struggle to recall even previously learned information when it is overwhelmed with last-minute study. Also, the urgent nature of cramming and the stress placed on your brain contribute to anxiety. You'll be more likely to go to the test feeling unprepared and having trouble thinking clearly.

So don't cram, and don't stay up late before the test, even just to review your notes at a leisurely pace. Your brain needs rest more than it needs to go over the information again. In fact, plan to finish your studies by noon or early afternoon the day before the test. Give your brain the rest of the day to relax or focus on other things, and get a good night's sleep. Then you will be fresh for the test and better able to recall what you've studied.

Step 6: Take a practice test

Many courses offer sample tests, either online or in the study materials. This is an excellent resource to check whether you have mastered the material, as well as to prepare for the test format and environment.

Check the test format ahead of time: the number of questions, the type (multiple choice, free response, etc.), and the time limit. Then create a plan for working through them. For example, if you have 30 minutes to take a 60-question test, your limit is 30 seconds per question. Spend less time on the questions you know well so that you can take more time on the difficult ones.

If you have time to take several practice tests, take the first one open book, with no time limit. Work through the questions at your own pace and make sure you fully understand them. Gradually work up to taking a test under test conditions: sit at a desk with all study materials put away and set a timer. Pace yourself to make sure you finish the test with time to spare and go back to check your answers if you have time.

After each test, check your answers. On the questions you missed, be sure you understand why you missed them. Did you misread the question (tests can use tricky wording)? Did you forget the information? Or was it something you hadn't learned? Go back and study any shaky areas that the practice tests reveal.

Taking these tests not only helps with your grade, but also aids in combating test anxiety. If you're already used to the test conditions, you're less likely to worry about it, and working through tests until you're scoring well gives you a confidence boost. Go through the practice tests until you feel comfortable, and then you can go into the test knowing that you're ready for it.

Test Tips

On test day, you should be confident, knowing that you've prepared well and are ready to answer the questions. But aside from preparation, there are several test day strategies you can employ to maximize your performance.

First, as stated before, get a good night's sleep the night before the test (and for several nights before that, if possible). Go into the test with a fresh, alert mind rather than staying up late to study.

Try not to change too much about your normal routine on the day of the test. It's important to eat a nutritious breakfast, but if you normally don't eat breakfast at all, consider eating just a protein bar. If you're a coffee drinker, go ahead and have your normal coffee. Just make sure you time it so that the caffeine doesn't wear off right in the middle of your test. Avoid sugary beverages, and drink enough water to stay hydrated but not so much that you need a restroom break 10 minutes into the test. If your test isn't first thing in the morning, consider going for a walk or doing a light workout before the test to get your blood flowing.

Allow yourself enough time to get ready, and leave for the test with plenty of time to spare so you won't have the anxiety of scrambling to arrive in time. Another reason to be early is to select a good seat. It's helpful to sit away from doors and windows, which can be distracting. Find a good seat, get out your supplies, and settle your mind before the test begins.

When the test begins, start by going over the instructions carefully, even if you already know what to expect. Make sure you avoid any careless mistakes by following the directions.

Then begin working through the questions, pacing yourself as you've practiced. If you're not sure on an answer, don't spend too much time on it, and don't let it shake your confidence. Either skip it and come back later, or eliminate as many wrong answers as possible and guess among the remaining ones. Don't dwell on these questions as you continue—put them out of your mind and focus on what lies ahead.

Be sure to read all of the answer choices, even if you're sure the first one is the right answer. Sometimes you'll find a better one if you keep reading. But don't second-guess yourself if you do immediately know the answer. Your gut instinct is usually right. Don't let test anxiety rob you of the information you know.

If you have time at the end of the test (and if the test format allows), go back and review your answers. Be cautious about changing any, since your first instinct tends to be correct, but make sure you didn't misread any of the questions or accidentally mark the wrong answer choice. Look over any you skipped and make an educated guess.

At the end, leave the test feeling confident. You've done your best, so don't waste time worrying about your performance or wishing you could change anything. Instead, celebrate the successful completion of this test. And finally, use this test to learn how to deal with anxiety even better next time.

Review Video: 5 Tips to Beat Test Anxiety
Visit mometrix.com/academy and enter code: 570656

Important Qualification

Not all anxiety is created equal. If your test anxiety is causing major issues in your life beyond the classroom or testing center, or if you are experiencing troubling physical symptoms related to your anxiety, it may be a sign of a serious physiological or psychological condition. If this sounds like your situation, we strongly encourage you to seek professional help.

Thank You

We at Mometrix would like to extend our heartfelt thanks to you, our friend and patron, for allowing us to play a part in your journey. It is a privilege to serve people from all walks of life who are unified in their commitment to building the best future they can for themselves.

The preparation you devote to these important testing milestones may be the most valuable educational opportunity you have for making a real difference in your life. We encourage you to put your heart into it—that feeling of succeeding, overcoming, and yes, conquering will be well worth the hours you've invested.

We want to hear your story, your struggles and your successes, and if you see any opportunities for us to improve our materials so we can help others even more effectively in the future, please share that with us as well. **The team at Mometrix would be absolutely thrilled to hear from you!** So please, send us an email (support@mometrix.com) and let's stay in touch.

If you'd like some additional help, check out these other resources we offer for your exam:

http://MometrixFlashcards.com/Series3

Additional Bonus Material

Due to our efforts to try to keep this book to a manageable length, we've created a link that will give you access to all of your additional bonus material.

Please visit https://www.mometrix.com/bonus948/series3 to access the information.